HODDER GCSE HISTORY FC

HENRY VIII AND HIS MINISTERS

1509–40

Dale Scarboro • Ian Dawson

DYNAMIC LEARNING

HODDER EDUCATION
LEARN MORE

Note: The wording and sentence structure of some written sources have been adapted and simplified to make them accessible to all pupils while faithfully preserving the sense of the original.

Every effort has been made to trace all copyright holders, but if any have been inadvertently overlooked, the Publishers will be pleased to make the necessary arrangements at the first opportunity.

Although every effort has been made to ensure that website addresses are correct at time of going to press, Hodder Education cannot be held responsible for the content of any website mentioned in this book. It is sometimes possible to find a relocated web page by typing in the address of the home page for a website in the URL window of your browser.

Hachette UK's policy is to use papers that are natural, renewable and recyclable products and made from wood grown in sustainable forests. The logging and manufacturing processes are expected to conform to the environmental regulations of the country of origin.

Orders: please contact Bookpoint Ltd, 130 Milton Park, Abingdon, Oxon OX14 4SB. Telephone: (44) 01235 827720. Fax: (44) 01235 400454. Email education@bookpoint.co.uk Lines are open from 9 a.m. to 5 p.m., Monday to Saturday, with a 24-hour message answering service. You can also order through our website: www.hoddereducation.co.uk

ISBN: 978 1 4718 6178 9

© Dale Scarboro and Ian Dawson 2016

First published in 2016 by
Hodder Education,
An Hachette UK Company
Carmelite House
50 Victoria Embankment
London EC4Y 0DZ

www.hoddereducation.co.uk

Impression number 10 9 8 7 6 5 4 3 2 1

Year   2019 2018 2017 2016

Cover photo © 2003 Topham Picturepoint/TopFoto; © World History Archive/TopFoto

Illustrations by DC Graphic Design Limited, Barking Dog Art, Cartoon Studio Ltd, Oxford Designers and Illustrators, Peter Lubach, Tony Randell

Typeset in ITC Legacy Serif Std Book 10/12pt by DC Graphic Design Limited, Hextable, Kent.

Printed in Italy

A catalogue record for this title is available from the British Library.

CONTENTS

1 Was Henry VIII really a great and successful king?

1.1 What do you already know about Henry VIII?

Henry VIII is the most famous monarch in English history. When people think about Henry VIII, the picture on the opposite page is the image almost everyone has in their minds. This is Henry in 1536 when he was 45 years old, seemingly at the height of his majesty and power. This portrait is certainly intended to portray Henry as a great king, a king whom no one would dare to challenge, a king whose successes rang around Europe.

This book explores whether Henry really was a great and successful king. The activities on this page identify what you already know and think about Henry.

CURRENT IDEAS ABOUT HENRY VIII

1. Work with a partner. Complete a mind map like the one below with as much information as you already have about Henry VIII. Use your memory, not books. The best way to start is to jot everything down in rough, then organise it into a pattern on the mind map. What, for example, might be the main themes or topics to go on the map?

2. Now think about your answer to the question below. Draw your own large version of the scales diagram below and add to it all the evidence you have on your mind map.

3. Write a short answer to the question on the mind map, identifying what you currently think about Henry. At the end of each section of the book you will have the chance to review your answer.

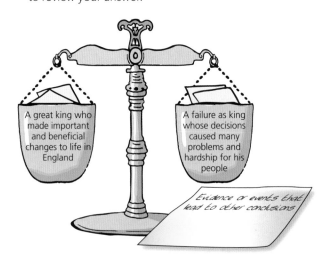

Anne Boleyn

Wives

Was Henry VIII really a great and successful King?

A great king who made important and beneficial changes to life in England

A failure as king whose decisions caused many problems and hardship for his people

Evidence or events that lead to other conclusions

Identifying what you already think

It may seem strange to begin by answering the question that acts as the main thread in this book. However, it is always important to identify what you already know – or think you know – when you begin a new topic. This can give you confidence that you do have some useful knowledge already. It also identifies your 'preconceptions', the ideas you have already (for example, you may think that Henry was hugely successful). Research suggests that, unless you identify these ideas, they can stay in your mind and dominate the way you think about the topic even if the evidence suggests you may be wrong. So be careful – keep thinking and remember that in History it is OK to change your mind as you learn more.

◀ Henry VIII, as he looked around 1536. This portrait was painted at some time later in the 1500s but is closely based on a painting completed around 1536 by Hans Holbein, the greatest painter of the time. The original portrait was destroyed in a fire in 1698, but many copies were made in Henry's lifetime.

1.2 A story of glory and success?

The timeline below shows the main events of Henry's reign. It probably includes events that you included in your concept map on page 2, but there is also new information and events.

We need criteria to help us decide whether Henry was a success. Here are four criteria – the things people in the 1500s saw as evidence of a successful monarch.

a) Did Henry defend his country from foreign threats? (Or did he create those threats?)

b) Did Henry unite his people over religion? (Or did he create religious divisions?)

c) Did he help his people live peacefully and prosperously? (Or did his decisions lead to rebellions and greater poverty?)

d) Did he make sure he had a clear successor? (Or did he increase fears of civil war breaking out over the crown when he died?)

There is also one more criterion to add, the one that was probably most important to Henry himself. He became king aged 17 and, like many young men, he wanted fame and glory. So this fifth criterion is:

e) Did Henry win fame and glory for himself?

1509–19

1509 Henry married Catherine of Aragon, the widow of his dead brother, Arthur. Such a marriage would normally have been prohibited but was allowed by the Pope on the grounds that Catherine and Arthur had not had sexual intercourse and so had not consummated their marriage.

1510 Thomas Wolsey appointed to the **Privy Council** (Henry's advisers).

1512–14 War with France. Henry had some success but the war was very expensive and he was let down by his allies.

1513 War with Scotland. King James IV of Scotland was killed at the Battle of Flodden. Henry was in France at the time.

1514–18 Henry wanted to renew war with France but could not persuade any other country to join him.

1515 Thomas Wolsey was appointed **Chancellor** of England and became Henry's **Chief Minister**.

1520–29

1520 Henry met King Francis of France near Calais at the Field of Cloth of Gold, a great diplomatic event that seemed to show off Henry's power.

1521 The Pope gave Henry the title 'Defender of the Faith' for writing a book defending the Pope and the Catholic Church against criticisms by Martin Luther, a German priest.

1522–5 War with France. Nothing was achieved, at great expense.

1525 The Amicable Grant Rising: a rebellion in East Anglia caused by high taxes.

1526–9 Henry wanted to end his marriage to Catherine so he could marry Anne Boleyn. All efforts to persuade the Pope to grant an **annulment** failed.

1528 Henry declared war on Emperor Charles V of Germany, but no war was actually fought.

1529 Wolsey fell from power over his failure to persuade the Pope to grant an annulment of Henry's marriage to Catherine of Aragon. Wolsey died on his way to stand trial for **treason**.

HENRY VIII – THE STORY IN OUTLINE

1. Look at each of the criteria on page 4 in turn and read the information on these two pages. How successful do you think Henry was in achieving each criterion? Did he achieve:
   a) consistent outstanding success
   b) occasional success
   c) very little success
   d) no success at all?

2. Choose two events that suggest that Henry was a great and successful king. Explain your choices.

3. Choose two events that challenge the view that Henry was a great and successful king. Explain your choices.

4. Work with a partner. Your task is to tell the outline story of Henry's reign from 1509 to 1540 in one minute – you can say a lot in one minute! Plan the story using your answers to Questions 1 and 2 and include your verdict on whether Henry seems to have been a success. Then write out your story.

1530–40

1531 Thomas Cromwell became Henry's Chief Minister. He masterminded setting up the Church of England and ending English ties to the Roman Catholic Church.

1532 The clergy (priests, bishops, archbishops in the English Church) accepted the King and not the Pope as their lawmaker.

1532 Anne Boleyn became pregnant. For her child to be heir to the throne, Henry had to divorce Catherine and marry Anne before the birth.

1533 Henry married Anne Boleyn, who was crowned Queen of England. Their daughter Elizabeth was born.

1534 The Act of Supremacy said Henry was the Head of the Church of England. All monks and nuns were required to take an oath accepting Henry as Head of the Church. The break with the Roman Catholic Church was complete.

1535 John Fisher, Bishop of Rochester, and Sir Thomas More, Henry's former Lord Chancellor, were executed for refusing to recognise Henry as the Head of the Church of England.

1536 Parliament passed an Act for the Dissolution (destruction) of the lesser Monasteries. Many monasteries had given help to the poor and sick.

1536 Anne Boleyn was executed for treason. Henry married Jane Seymour.

1536 A widespread rebellion broke out in the north – the Pilgrimage of Grace. The rebels were protesting against the **Dissolution of the Monasteries**. After seeming to make concessions, Henry had the leaders executed.

1537 Birth of Edward, Henry's male heir. Death of Jane Seymour.

1538–9 Fear of invasion of England by Charles V and the King of France in order to restore Catholicism.

1539 Dissolution of larger monasteries.

1540 January Henry married Anne of Cleves.

July Thomas Cromwell executed. Marriage to Anne of Cleves annulled. Henry married Catherine Howard.

1.3 Who's who in the story of Henry VIII?

You will meet many people in this book and you need to know more than just their names. You need to know what they did and the impact they had on events during Henry's reign. This information is essential for explaining why things happened as they did.

You will not remember every individual straightaway, but you can make a good start by completing the activity below and then keeping working at remembering who's who. After a while, you'll be surprised how well you know 'who's who' but, if you get confused, turn back to these pages to remind yourself of the key individuals.

WHO WAS WHO IN HENRY'S REIGN?

1. Draw your own copy of the Who's Who? chart below. Find out what each person did by looking them up in this book and add a brief description to your chart. You could include their relationship to Henry, whether they supported or opposed him, and what they did that was important.

2. If there is something special about a person's relationship with Henry write that along a ribbon, like the one done for you.

Prince Edward

Jane Seymour

Anne of Cleves

Catherine Howard

Catherine of Aragon

Henry's first wife

Henry VIII

Anne Boleyn

Princess Mary

Princess Elizabeth

The Pope

Emperor Charles V

Francis I of France

Thomas Wolsey

Thomas Cromwell

Elizabeth Barton

John Fisher

Sir Thomas More

You could do this activity physically in the classroom, using ribbons or string, with each of you 'playing' one of the characters and telling the others who you are, which other people you are connected to and what your role was in Henry's reign. By adopting these characters at the beginning of your course, your teacher will then be able to move you around to form different groupings as and when appropriate.

Confusion warning

Some of the people in this book had more than one name, because they also had a title. For example, Thomas Howard was Duke of Norfolk, Thomas Cranmer was the Archbishop of Canterbury, Sir Thomas More was Lord Chancellor. The Emperor Charles V was the Emperor of Germany and King of Spain and Duke of Burgundy. When you are making your notes about these people, you need to be very careful to note all the names and titles they were known by. Some books will refer to these people by their titles alone, others by their names. You need to keep track!

Elizabeth Barton and Robert Aske are not drawn in detail here because we do not know exactly what they looked like.

Duke of Norfolk

Thomas Cranmer

Robert Aske

ASKING GOOD QUESTIONS

One vital historical skill is the ability to ask good questions. What questions do you want to ask about the events of Henry's reign on pages 4–5, or the people shown on these pages?

Use the question starters shown as prompts for your questions.

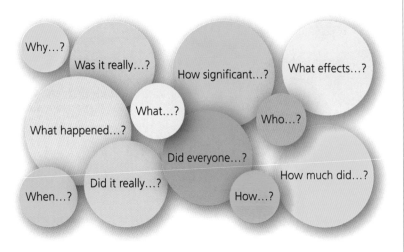

Why…? Was it really…? How significant…? What effects…? What…? What happened…? Who…? Did everyone…? How much did…? When…? Did it really…? How…?

Visible learning: Getting better at History – why are we making learning visible?

This book does not just tell you about Henry VIII and his reign. It also helps you get better at History and achieve the best possible grade in your exam. We have already begun on pages 6–7 by highlighting the importance of identifying all the key individuals and giving you tasks to get to know them. Confusing individuals is a common mistake students make.

However, what do you do when you meet new information and feel puzzled? This is what to do:

> Think about why you're puzzled and **identify** the problem. Then admit there's something you don't understand and tell your teacher. The result – your teacher helps you sort out the problem, your confidence increases and you do well in your exams.

Admitting you are puzzled means you are taking responsibility for your own learning and your own success. We emphasised one very important word – identify. You cannot get better at History unless you identify exactly what you don't understand. To put that another way, you have to make a problem visible before you can put it right.

The value of visible learning

The things we get wrong and then correct are often the things we remember best because we've had to think harder about them. Saying 'I don't understand' is the first step towards getting it right.

1.4 The importance of religion in the early 1500s

Another common mistake made by students is to underestimate the importance of religion in the sixteenth century. Many people died during Henry's reign because of their devotion to their religion.

Angels weighing the souls of the dead

Ladder to Heaven with sinners failing to climb to Heaven

Devils boiling murderers over a fire

THE IMPORTANCE OF RELIGION ?

1 Which events on pages 4–5 demonstrate the importance of religious beliefs to people?

2 What is the message in this painting?

3 How does the painting help to explain why people were prepared to die for their religious beliefs?

▲ Medieval churches displayed paintings of the **Last Judgement** where people could see them throughout services. The message was clear – people who had led good lives went to heaven to be with Jesus for eternity, but the torments of hell awaited all sinners and people who did not follow the right religion. People in the sixteenth century believed that their souls would go to heaven and hell for all of eternity, depending on how they had behaved in this life.

The beliefs and features of the Roman Catholic Church

By the time Henry became king in 1509 England had been a Catholic country for nearly a thousand years. Religion played a central part in daily life. Most people went to church every Sunday and all the important rituals of their lives were linked to the Church, including baptisms, marriage, holy days and harvest festivals. The Church was the centre of community life and supported the people through hardship. Many people were employed by monasteries, which also provided food and other help for the poor and elderly. Religion also gave people hope, not only during this life, but by teaching that leading a good life would ensure eternal salvation. Not surprisingly, people thought their beliefs were the right ones and all others were wrong.

Decoration and music

The appearance of the church was almost as important to people as the type of service they listened to. Catholic churches were built to show the glory and majesty of God and were as elaborate and expensive as possible. They were filled with stained glass windows, statues, pictures, murals, wood and marble carvings and were dominated by huge altars and organs. Many people, not only the rich, left money in their wills for church decorations.

The head of the Church

The Pope in Rome was head of the Church. There was also a hierarchy of cardinals, archbishops and bishops to help the Pope govern the Church. Therefore, in theory, English people were expected to be loyal to both their monarch and the Pope.

The Roman Catholic Church

Priests and their robes

Catholic priests wore richly decorated robes called vestments. This was an important part of celebrating God.

Church services

The Bible was only available in Latin and read only by priests. Church services were also in Latin, even though people did not understand the words. They were used to hearing and repeating the rhythms of the words and took comfort from this tradition. Catholics believed that a miracle took place during Mass when the bread and wine given to the people were turned into the body and blood of Jesus through the powers of the priest.

THE ROMAN CATHOLIC CHURCH

Complete a diagram like the one below, summarising the key features of the Roman Catholic religion.

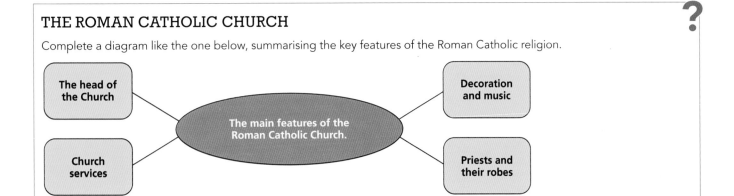

The head of the Church — The main features of the Roman Catholic Church. — Decoration and music

Church services — Priests and their robes

Henry VIII and Wolsey, 1509–29

This first section (Chapters 2 to 4) explores the first twenty years of Henry's reign, assessing in detail how successful he was. This page introduces some of the major decisions Henry faced and offers a set of options for you to choose from. Which ones would you have chosen if, like Henry, your heart was set on achieving glory? Remember that in 1509 Henry was only 17 years old. Nowadays he would have been trying on his new crown while beginning the countdown to his A levels!

Visible learning

The value of decision-making activities

This is the first decision-making activity in the book. You will meet others later on. These activities may just seem like fun but fun is not the aim! These decision-making activities help you learn more effectively because:

a) thinking carefully about which choice to make helps you understand the situation more thoroughly and helps embed it in your memory. Information has more chance of sticking in your memory if you are interested in and enjoy the task.

b) thinking about the choices people had helps you understand that choices were difficult and events could have turned out differently. They were not inevitable. This gives you better understanding of the complexity of situations.

REMEMBER – in decision-making activities it is not the choice itself that helps you learn, but thinking about and explaining your choice.

DECISION 1: 1509 – CHOOSING YOUR COUNCILLORS

Your father, King Henry VII, died with a reputation for greed. Some of his councillors are hated for extorting high taxes from people. Should you:

a make a clean start with completely new councillors?

b keep most of your father's councillors but punish (perhaps even execute) the most unpopular individuals?

c keep all your father's councillors because you need their experience?

DECISION 2: 1509 – FRANCE: WAR OR PEACE?

France is England's oldest enemy. You enjoy jousting tournaments and reading about war. Will you:

a continue your father's policy of avoiding war as much as possible? Your father's councillors oppose war with France – they say it is dangerous and expensive.

b invade France with your army immediately?

c plan a war when you have secured the right alliances, perhaps with Spain, so you are not fighting France alone?

DECISION 3: 1516 – WHAT TO DO ABOUT WOLSEY?

There is a great deal of gossip and opposition to your Chief Minister, Thomas Wolsey. Men say he has become far too powerful and that his power makes you, the king, look weak to your own people and to foreign rulers, especially to the King of France. Should you:

a dismiss Wolsey to show who is truly king? You cannot afford to look weak as it will lead to the danger of invasion or rebellion.

b ignore the talk because Wolsey is very valuable to you? He does all the hard work you do not want to do. Besides which, you know that you are in control whatever people think.

DECISION 4: 1518 – WHAT ROLE WILL YOU PLAY IN EUROPE?

The two most powerful states in Europe are France and the Holy Roman Empire. They have been at war, but now Wolsey wants you to mediate between them to produce a peace treaty. Should you:

a agree with this plan because it will show off your own power? You will look like the key figure in Europe, so powerful that you can persuade France and the Empire to make peace.

b dismiss the plan because there is nothing glorious in peace? Great kings fight wars and win battles. It would be better to make an alliance with either France or the Empire and to fight the other one and win a glorious war.

DECISION 5: 1525 – HOW WILL YOU DEAL WITH THE REBELS?

You need money for war with France. Wolsey has demanded that people pay a tax which he has called a 'friendly gift' of money! This tax is very unpopular. People throughout the country have tried to avoid paying it and people are gathering with weapons in East Anglia to fight the tax collectors. It looks like a rebellion. Will you:

a abandon collecting the tax and pardon the leaders of the rebellion?

b send in your soldiers to capture and execute the rebels so you do not look weak?

THOMAS WOLSEY, THE KING'S CHIEF MINISTER

Wolsey was a remarkable man. People expected the King's advisers to be noblemen but Wolsey was the son of a butcher. He became one of the King's advisers because he was extremely clever, efficient and hard-working. He joined the King's council in 1510 (when he was 38 years old) and became the King's Chief Minister in 1515.

This 1567 portrait of Wolsey by Jacques Le Boucq is a copy of a drawing made around 1515–20.

DECISION 6: 1529 – WHO WILL SOLVE YOUR MARRIAGE PROBLEM?

You want the Pope to annul your marriage to Catherine of Aragon so you can marry Anne Boleyn. However, Wolsey has failed to persuade the Pope to end your marriage to Catherine. Wolsey's enemies, including some powerful noblemen, say he has not been working hard enough to persuade the Pope. Should you:

a dismiss Wolsey? This will show the Pope and everyone else that you are determined to end the marriage.

b keep Wolsey as your Chief Minister? He has been your leading minister for fifteen years and deserves your support for all his hard work.

c demote Wolsey from Chief Minister but keep him as your chief adviser behind the scenes?

HENRY'S DECISIONS 1509–29

1. You will find the decisions Henry made on pages 14–15. Award points for choosing the same decisions as Henry. Who has the highest score in your class?

2. Which decision was the most straightforward for you and which the most difficult? Explain why you made those decisions.

3. What have you learned about Henry from the decisions he made?

4. Choose two words that you think sum up Henry's character from what you have learned from these decisions.

2 Did Henry have the potential to be a great king?

2.1 'Renaissance Prince'

Henry is often described as a 'Renaissance Prince'. The Renaissance was the period of history around 1400 to 1550 when new discoveries were being made, and when new ideas were spreading rapidly. Therefore, a 'Renaissance Prince' was a ruler who was interested in new ideas and had a wide range of talents – the kind of man with the potential to be a great king.

One English nobleman, Lord Mountjoy, certainly thought Henry would make a great king. In May 1509, when Henry had only been king for a month, Mountjoy wrote in a letter:

> King Henry is a prince with exceptional and almost more than human talents. How courageously and wisely he is acting, what a passion he has for justice and honesty, how warmly he welcomes men of intelligence. How excited everyone is here and we are all congratulating ourselves on the new King's greatness. Heaven smiles, earth rejoices...

This chapter explores whether Mountjoy was right about Henry's potential as king. As you read pages 12–17, collect evidence in a copy of the table below about Henry's potential to be a great king.

Evidence suggesting Henry could become a great king	Evidence raising doubts about whether Henry would become a great king

Visible learning

Knowledge Organisers

The table is the first example of a Knowledge Organiser in this book. Another common mistake students make is to make such detailed notes that they cannot find the main points they need. Knowledge Organisers focus on recording the key points you need. You can then make separate, more detailed notes to support the key points in the Knowledge Organiser.

The Tudor family

Henry Tudor (who became Henry VII) did not expect to be king. He was very distantly related to the royal family, but from the age of 14 to 27 he lived abroad in exile. Then there was a rebellion against King Richard III and the rebels needed a leader as an alternative king. They chose Henry. In 1485 he invaded England and killed Richard III at the Battle of Bosworth.

However, Henry VII also had to fight off rebels so there was uncertainty during much of his reign about whether the Tudors would be able to keep the crown. In addition, two of Henry VII's sons died young, as the family tree below shows, leaving only Henry to follow his father as king. If Henry died too, then that would be the end of the Tudors as the royal family. This uncertainty may well have affected Henry VIII and made him anxious about rebellions even after he became king.

This family tree shows ► Henry VIII's family. They are the famous Tudor family, although no one in the 1500s ever referred to them as 'the Tudors'. They did not need a family name as they were the kings and queens.

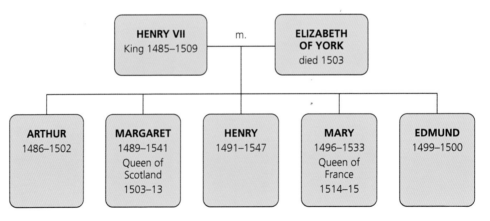

HENRY VII — King 1485–1509 — m. — ELIZABETH OF YORK — died 1503

ARTHUR 1486–1502 | MARGARET 1489–1541 Queen of Scotland 1503–13 | HENRY 1491–1547 | MARY 1496–1533 Queen of France 1514–15 | EDMUND 1499–1500

Young Henry and his accession

> This day is the end of sadness, the beginning of joy.

Those were the words of Sir Thomas More about the beginning of Henry VIII's reign in April 1509. The 'sadness' had been the final dull years of Henry VII's reign. The 'joy' was the feeling of celebration because a young, talented prince was now king. The extracts on this page provide reports by other people who met Henry during the early years of his reign.

A   From a report by Pasqualigo, the Venetian ambassador to England in April 1515

The King is the handsomest prince I have ever set eyes on. He is above the usual height with a finely shaped leg, his complexion very fair and bright, with auburn hair combed straight and short in the French fashion and a round face so very beautiful that it would become a pretty woman, his throat being rather long and thick. He speaks French, English and Latin and a little Italian, plays well on the lute and harpsichord, sings from book at sight, draws the bow with greater strength than any man in England and jousts marvellously.

B   From a report by Giustinian, the Venetian ambassador to England in April 1519

King Henry was very religious, attended services three times a day when he hunted and sometimes five on other days. He was extremely fond of hunting and never stopped riding until he had tired eight or ten horses. He was also fond of tennis, at which it was the prettiest thing in the world to see him play, his fair skin glowing through a shirt of the finest texture.

C   A comment by Sir Thomas More, Henry's Lord Chancellor, to his son-in-law, William Roper. Roper wrote _A Life of Sir Thomas More_ in 1535, after More was executed.

I find the King a very good lord and I believe he favours me as much as any other subject within the whole country. However if he could win a castle in France by cutting my head off then my head would be sure to go.

▲ This portrait of Henry VIII was painted in 1520 when he was 29 years old. He thoroughly enjoyed and was very good at archery and jousting. In 1515 he was described as excelling all others at jousting and 'looked like St George on horseback'. He also composed music, played several instruments and enjoyed discussing astronomy and mathematics with experts.

THE YOUNG KING

1. Use the information on these pages to list Henry's talents and skills.
2. What can you learn about Henry's character from these pages?
3. Create your own copy of the table on page 12. Use the information on these pages to begin adding evidence to your table. Remember that you are not just listing his talents but selecting details that provide evidence of his potential to be a great king.

2.2 King, monarchy and country

THE KING AND HIS COUNTRY ?

1. Work in pairs to read pages 14–15 and answer the questions on the bingo card below.
   a) Your first task is to complete a line of questions – the first pair to do this correctly wins.
   b) Second, compete to see which pair is the first to get a full house of correct answers.
2. Return to your table from page 12. What evidence or information can you now add to this?

1 Why was appearance important to kings?	2 Identify two reasons why success in war against France would be difficult.	3 Why did Henry fear that rebellions might break out?
4 Identify three aims that Henry had as a young king.	5 Give two reasons why Henry was keen to go to war with France.	6 Identify two pieces of evidence from pages 13–15 that show Henry could be ruthless.
7 How important was the King's role in government?	8 Why was the influence of the Pope in England a 'grey area'?	9 Identify two of Henry's aims that he could not completely control.

EXPECTATIONS OF A KING

As King, Henry was expected to:

■ defend his people from foreign threats, increase England's power and lead his army himself
■ show off England's wealth and power through his own rich appearance
■ make sure people lived peacefully and prosperously, preventing rebellions and law-breaking
■ respect and unite his nobles so they supported him and helped him govern the country
■ defend the Church and unite his people in one religion
■ father male children so there were no doubts about who was his heir.

▲ The young King Henry

HENRY'S APPEARANCE AND CHARACTER

Henry's appearance was important if he was to be successful. People expected a king to look impressive, to show off the wealth and power of his country, and Henry certainly looked like a great leader. His interests, such as jousting, hunting and sports, were also important because they were activities his nobles thought were important and could share with the King. This would help unite the nobles and the King.

Henry could also be ruthless. Decision 1 on page 10 asked what he should do about his father's councillors. He kept most of them to begin with, but within days of becoming king he ordered the arrest of two of the most unpopular councillors, Empson and Dudley, and then had them put on trial and executed. This showed that Henry could be ruthless to win support and popularity.

HENRY'S AIMS

As a young man, Henry's main aim was to win glory and power for himself and England by waging successful wars against France. He had read histories of past wars with France and his heroes were great warrior kings such as Edward III and Henry V, who had beaten French armies in famous battles.

Henry also wanted to prevent rebellions breaking out as they had done when his father was king. Having sons to secure the line of succession would be important in this.

And he wanted to enjoy being king!

HENRY'S PERSONAL STYLE OF MONARCHY

Henry believed in traditional ways of doing things – he was very conservative in his attitudes. He believed that the monarchy was all-powerful. Therefore he had a very personal style of government in which he took all the important decisions about how the country was run – decisions such as going to war and whom to appoint to important jobs. He expected to be obeyed because God had chosen him to be king and rule England. However there was nothing new about this, as all previous kings had had the same personal style of governing.

HENRY'S VIEWS ON SOVEREIGNTY AND MONARCHY

As monarch, Henry was 'sovereign' within England – which meant that no one else shared his power. In theory the Pope, as Head of the Catholic Church, also had power over the archbishops, bishops, monasteries and priests, but this was a 'grey area'. In practice, Henry expected that he himself would choose the archbishops and bishops and that the Pope would accept his decisions. Henry also expected that, in return for his own support for the Church, the Pope would agree to any requests Henry made.

HENRY'S POTENTIAL STRENGTHS AND WEAKNESSES AS KING

Henry had many strengths – his youth, his appearance and glamour, his enthusiasm for war and sports which appealed to his nobles. He was intelligent and he seemed to provide a fresh, optimistic start after the fears and worries of his father's reign. At the same time, Henry did not want to change the way kings behaved or governed – his style as king was very much the same as kings in the past who had been successful.

Therefore, Henry did not appear to have any weaknesses when he became king, except that he did not have any experience of being king. His weaknesses would only appear as time went by and they depended on how he responded to things that he could not control – the power of other countries, the willingness of his people to pay taxes to cover the cost of his wars, whether he fathered male heirs, whether good harvests gave his people enough to eat.

ENGLAND'S POWER ABROAD

In the early 1400s England had ruled half of France, but that empire had been lost by the 1450s. The French town of Calais was now the only part of France that England still possessed – a gateway for trade between England and the continent. France was a much larger and richer country than England and Kings of France were now more interested in winning land and wealth in Italy than in war with England. If Henry wanted to fight a successful and glorious war he would need strong allies to take on mighty France.

2.3 England in 1509: Society and government

Society

In 1509 the population was beginning to grow again after the impact of the Black Death of 1348 and further outbreaks of plague. There were around 2 ¼ million people in England and Wales, about the same as in Greater Manchester today. Most lived in villages – in timber-framed houses. Towns were small, huddled within their walls; at night, town gates were closed. Everyone's health and prosperity depended on the quality of each year's harvest. A poor harvest meant people went hungry. Two or three successive bad harvests led to illness, even death from starvation.

The number of people who could read had increased a lot in the 1400s and the invention of printing made books more widely available. There was a great deal of trade with Europe, mostly in cloth and wool. These contacts meant that the English borrowed many ideas from Europe – Flemish fashions, Italian music, German art.

God

The King
(God's chosen representative)

Nobles
(great landowners)

Gentry
(lesser landowners)

Wealthy merchants

Yeomen
(farmers who owned land)

Tenant farmers
(who rented land from a landowner)

Craftspeople, labourers, servants, the unemployed

The standard of living was generally high because the small population meant there was plenty of work – meat was common fare even in a poor household. In a rich establishment like a nobleman's castle or the Royal Court, the two daily meals could each easily run to twelve courses.

Society was still very structured or hierarchical, as seen in the diagram above. People were expected to know their place in society, but it was possible for people to rise up the levels, as the careers of Henry's ministers, Wolsey and Cromwell, show.

Government

The King

The King made all the key decisions such as whether to go to war, whom to appoint as his councillors and to important jobs, and when Parliament should meet. However, the King was expected to listen to advice from his councillors, especially the leading nobles.

▼ This diagram shows how the King's government was organised and who took part in it.

The Royal Household

The Household consisted of Henry and his family, and the servants needed to care for the royal family.

The Court

The Court consisted of the Household plus the King's friends and advisers. The Court and the Household were not physical buildings. They were groups of people. The Court was wherever the King chose to be.

The Council

The Council consisted of the men chosen by Henry to be his advisers. They were usually noblemen, senior members of the Church, and lawyers. The Council included the heads of government departments, such as the **Lord Treasurer**. Many men were advisers at one time or another, but usually meetings were attended by only a small number. They met frequently, sometimes daily, and were responsible for administration such as overseeing finances, meeting foreign ambassadors, drafting correspondence and controlling the business of Parliament.

Chief Ministers

Thomas Wolsey and Thomas Cromwell are often described as being Henry's Chief Ministers. They were Henry's leading advisers, took on huge amounts of work, did their best to solve the King's problems, and make the government work to achieve his aims. However, there was no official job with the title 'Chief Minister', and it is not a term that people used at the time. Historians use this term because it sums up neatly the roles of Wolsey and Cromwell.

Parliament

Parliament met when summoned by the King and ended when the King ordered it to end. Parliament's main role was to raise taxes for special occasions such as war. Therefore, Parliament did not meet every year and there could be several years between Parliaments. The members of the House of Commons were all wealthy men, landowning gentry or merchants from towns.

Nobles

There were around 60 or 70 nobles at any one time. They were the wealthiest landowners and had huge local influence. They expected to be the monarch's leading advisers, to deal with crime and social unrest locally, and to be commanders in wartime. Nobles could resent being left out of these tasks by a monarch, which, in the past, had led to rebellion on occasion.

Gentry

The gentry were important landowners in each county and some were very wealthy. The King needed the gentry to keep government running locally and to act as judges and sheriffs in each county. These roles were unpaid but gave the gentry great local status. Many were trained as lawyers and all were trained as soldiers and fought for the King if needed.

SOCIETY AND GOVERNMENT

1. What were the two greatest dangers to the health and prosperity of the people?
2. How did the size of the population influence prosperity?
3. Did the Council or Parliament play the more important part in government? Explain your choice.
4. What roles did:
   a) the nobles and
   b) the gentry play in government?
5. Return to your table from page 12. What evidence or information can you now add to your table? Think about the importance of Henry himself in choosing advisers and making decisions, and about what was outside Henry's control.
6. Did Henry have the potential to be a great king?
   a) Which of these phrases best sums up your view? (Or choose your own phrase.)

   certain to be a great king   highly likely to be a great king

   a good chance of being a great king   unlikely to be a great king

   b) Write a short answer explaining your choice of phrase.

3 Wolsey and his policies

3.1 The rise of Cardinal Wolsey, 1509–25

Wolsey's rise to power was remarkable. A butcher's son, born about 1471 in Ipswich, Wolsey was extraordinarily intelligent. His uncle, a wealthy merchant, probably paid for Thomas to be educated and attend Oxford University by the age of 15. He remained at the university and, in 1498, became a priest – a career in the Church was a good way for a clever young man to get on in life. Around 1501 Wolsey became chaplain to the Archbishop of Canterbury and quickly got to know other important men. In 1507 he was appointed a royal chaplain to King Henry VII, so now he was at Court. Wolsey soon showed his talents, rapidly and successfully carrying out diplomatic missions to several countries for the King.

When Henry VIII became king he appointed Wolsey to the Royal Council. In 1513, when Henry led an invasion of France, Wolsey was the brains behind the organisation of the army, its equipment and transport. His success was quickly rewarded. In 1514 he became Bishop of Lincoln and then Archbishop of York, the second most powerful position in the English Church. In 1515 the Pope appointed Wolsey a cardinal, the highest rank in the Catholic Church. There was nothing unusual in this – many English archbishops were made cardinals.

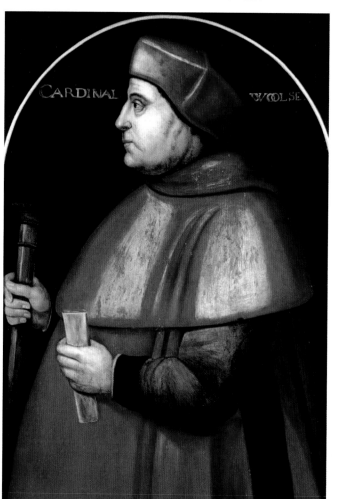

In 1515 King Henry appointed Wolsey Lord Chancellor of England, making Wolsey his Chief Minister (see page 11). For the next fourteen years, Wolsey led England's administration, keeping a firm grasp on both foreign and domestic policy.

HENRY'S FIRST WARS: FRANCE AND SCOTLAND, 1513

In 1513 Henry and his army invaded France, despite advice from his father's councillors that war was expensive and dangerous. Henry was not going to be put off winning glory! However, Henry's allies backed out of their agreement to attack France and his campaign fizzled out. He did win what was thrillingly called 'the Battle of the Spurs', although it was really only a small skirmish and pursuit of French cavalry. In contrast, Henry's general, the Earl of Surrey, won a decisive battle against the Scots at Flodden after the Scots invaded the north of England. The King of Scots and many of his nobles were killed. What turned out to be Henry's greatest victory was won when he was not there.

◀ A painting of Cardinal Wolsey dating from the 1520s. Wolsey was Henry VIII's Chief Minister from 1515 until 1529.

Wolsey: Roles, personality and wealth

For fifteen years Wolsey juggled the most demanding roles in England. As a cardinal and archbishop he was the leading churchman in England. However, his major role was as the King's Chief Minister, managing parliaments, raising taxes, leading diplomatic negotiations, planning military campaigns, drafting new laws and many other tasks. This meant that he did the hard work of government, allowing King Henry to spend his time jousting, hunting and in all his other many enjoyments.

Wolsey was able to juggle all this because he was highly intelligent, with great stamina and energy to work very long hours on the King's business. He was also deeply loyal to Henry. Among his other strengths were his skills as a negotiator and ability to charm and persuade people to agree with him. At other times he could lose his temper deliberately and use bad language to over-awe those who disagreed with him.

Wolsey also enjoyed and took pride in showing off his great wealth. By 1520 he was the King's wealthiest subject and spent his money lavishly on buildings, jewels, silver plate to decorate his houses, tapestries and clothing. This spending gave his rivals the opportunity to accuse him of extreme greed and of trying to rival the King's magnificence. However, it is important to remember that Wolsey was the King's leading adviser, an archbishop and cardinal. In these roles he was expected to live as magnificently as he could. He also needed a huge income to pay all the people who worked for him, including lawyers, administrators who did government business for him and all the different kinds of servants needed to keep his houses running.

WOLSEY'S RISE TO POWER

1. Select the four most important steps in Wolsey's rise to power and write them on your own copy of these steps, working up the steps in chronological order. Underneath, explain the significance of each step.

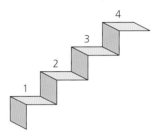

2. What qualities did Wolsey have that explain his rise to power?
3. Why was Wolsey so important to Henry?
4. What aspects of his personality and wealth led to criticism by his political rivals?
5. Create your own spider diagram to sum up Wolsey's roles, personality and wealth.

▼ Hampton Court Palace was a small house, rebuilt by Wolsey. There he lived in a style that his enemies said rivalled that of Henry himself. After Wolsey's death, Henry VIII took over Hampton Court and used it as a royal palace. To Wolsey's enemies, Hampton Court was the clearest evidence that the butcher's son thought he was the equal of the King.

3.2 England and Europe

One mistake students often make is that they over-estimate Henry's power in relation to other countries. This is because we usually think of Henry VIII as a very powerful ruler, a man who could do virtually anything he wished. This was true in England, but he was far less powerful in Europe. These pages help you to understand this – and to begin thinking about whether Henry's dream of military glory was ever likely to be achieved.

ENGLAND IN EUROPE ?

1. Why do you think population size and royal income were important for deciding the power of a country?

2. In what ways was England much weaker than France and the Holy Roman Empire?

3. If you were Wolsey advising King Henry would you advise him to:
   a) launch military campaigns against France to achieve glory?
   b) seek alliances as the best way to show that England can be powerful and important?

   Explain the reasons for your choice.

4. How strong were Henry's chances of achieving the military glory that he wanted?

Important vocabulary

Valois – the name of the royal family of France.

Hapsburg – the royal family of both Spain and the Holy Roman Empire (Germany).

Holy Roman Empire – a loose collection of over 300 German and north Italian states, ruled by an emperor elected by the princes of seven of these states.

Hapsburg-Valois War – the conflict between the King of France, Francis I, and Emperor Charles V of Germany, who was also King of Spain. The wars lasted on and off from 1521 to 1559.

Reformation – the period beginning in 1517 when the Christian Church in western Europe split in two, into the Catholic and Protestant Churches.

Papacy – the Pope and his territories: the Vatican in Rome and the Papal States in central Italy.

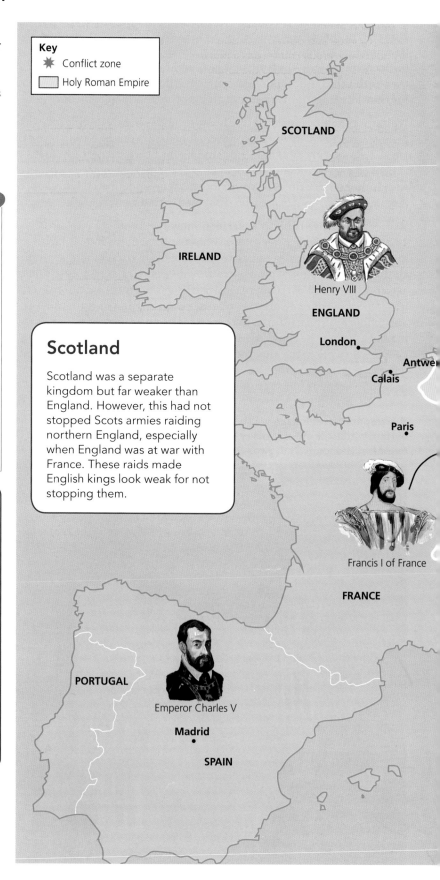

Key
✳ Conflict zone
☐ Holy Roman Empire

SCOTLAND

IRELAND

Henry VIII

ENGLAND

London

Antwe

Calais

Paris

Scotland

Scotland was a separate kingdom but far weaker than England. However, this had not stopped Scots armies raiding northern England, especially when England was at war with France. These raids made English kings look weak for not stopping them.

Francis I of France

FRANCE

PORTUGAL

Emperor Charles V

Madrid

SPAIN

France

The King of France, Francis I (1515-47), ruled a large and powerful kingdom. In the early 1400s France was a much smaller kingdom because the English had conquered much of northern France. By the 1450s, England had lost those lands and the kings of France had steadily rebuilt and extended their territory. Francis I was now fighting Emperor Charles V and the main war zone was northern Italy where both rulers hoped to gain wealthy territories.

- Population: 15 million
- Royal income: £350,000 per year

The Holy Roman Empire

Charles V ruled a wide range of territories:

a   The Austrian Empire in Germany and Hungary and the Duchy of Burgundy on France's eastern border. He inherited these lands in 1506 as heir of the ruling Hapsburg family.

b   In 1516 he became King of Spain, which included Naples and Sicily in Italy and had begun to conquer lands in Central and South America.

c   In 1519 he became Holy Roman Emperor in Germany. The Emperor did not directly govern the many states within the Empire but he was able to call on an imperial army and had enormous prestige.

- Population: 23 million
- Royal income: £560,000 per year

England

Henry VIII wanted to win glory in his foreign policy, but England was far less powerful than France and the Empire. Henry still claimed that he was the true King of France but his chances of repeating Henry V's conquest of France (1415-20) were non-existent. France and the Empire were interested in gaining the wealth of Italy, not in what was happening in England. His best hope of success lay in forming an alliance with either Francis or Charles in their war against each other. England's support might help one side win and, in the process, Henry might gain the glory and respect he craved.

- Population: 2.75 million
- Royal income: £110,000 per year
- Complicating factor: Henry VIII was married to Catherine of Aragon, the Spanish aunt of Emperor Charles V.

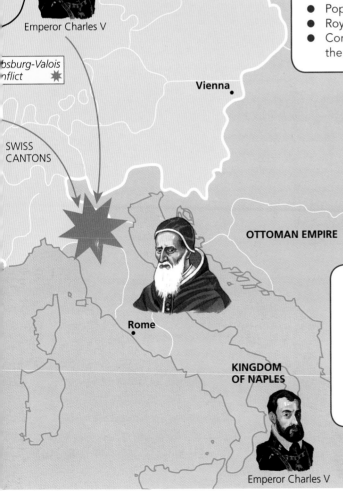

Emperor Charles V

bsburg-Valois nflict ✳

Vienna

SWISS CANTONS

OTTOMAN EMPIRE

Rome

KINGDOM OF NAPLES

Emperor Charles V

The Papacy

As the head of the Catholic Church throughout Europe the Pope had a unique power – the power of religion. By 1520 he faced a challenge from Martin Luther, a German-born critic of the papacy, but a split was far from inevitable and there was a chance that Luther and Rome might be reconciled. Both Francis I and Emperor Charles V looked to Rome for approval and diplomatic support.

Calais

The only part of France still governed by England. Calais was an important port. Many English merchants lived and worked there and it was strongly defended against French attack.

The Italian states

The country we call Italy was split into separate states with their own rules. These included the Papal States. France and the Empire were fighting to win control of northern Italy.

The Field of Cloth of Gold, 1520

You read on pages 20–21 that Henry's chances of achieving glory and success in Europe were poor. However, this painting (by an unknown artist) shows Henry in 1520 at the very centre of events, apparently on equal terms with King Francis I of France at the event called the Field of Cloth of Gold. What was this event?

In 1520 Wolsey arranged four royal meetings for Henry, two with Charles V and two with Francis I. The Field of Cloth of Gold was the most lavish and expensive meeting. Held just outside Calais, it lasted for over two weeks. It got its name from the gold thread woven into the fabric of three hundred French tents, the elaborate decorations and the beautiful armour and clothes worn by the participants. When the sunlight fell on this magnificent scene, it must have shimmered like a golden field. Most importantly, it made Henry appear to be one of the three great rulers in Europe, holding the fate of nations in his hands.

The two kings went to elaborate lengths to show how much they trusted each other. The site for the meeting was in a shallow valley so that neither king was camped higher than the other. King Francis dined with Henry's wife, Queen Catherine, while Henry dined with Francis's wife, Queen Claude. There were jousting tournaments, mock combat on foot, and fighting in pairs with spears and swords. The two kings apparently never jousted against each other, but they did fight in teams of noblemen. Unfortunately for Henry he did challenge Francis to a wrestling match, a contest Henry quickly lost.

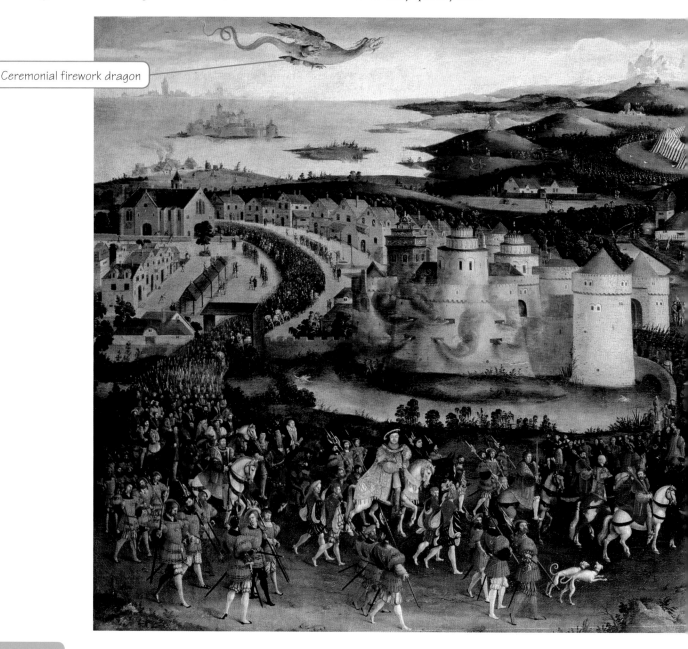

Ceremonial firework dragon

THE FIELD OF CLOTH OF GOLD

1. Identify the following features in the painting:
   a) A covered gallery where the kings and queens watched the jousting.
   b) The tiltyard where the jousting took place.
   c) A prefabricated wooden palace, made to look like stone.
   d) A fountain flowing with wine.
   e) The arrival of Henry VIII and Cardinal Wolsey.
2. Why do you think Henry VIII and Francis I never jousted against each other?
3. Why could Henry and Wolsey portray this event as a glorious success?
4. You are going to go on to assess the success of Henry and Wolsey's policies. What questions do you want to ask about the Field of Cloth of Gold to help you with this assessment?

You can watch a short video about Henry VIII's armour for the Field of Cloth of Gold, made by the Royal Armouries. Look for 'Henry VIII's foot combat armour for the Field of Cloth of Gold tournament in 1520' on YouTube.

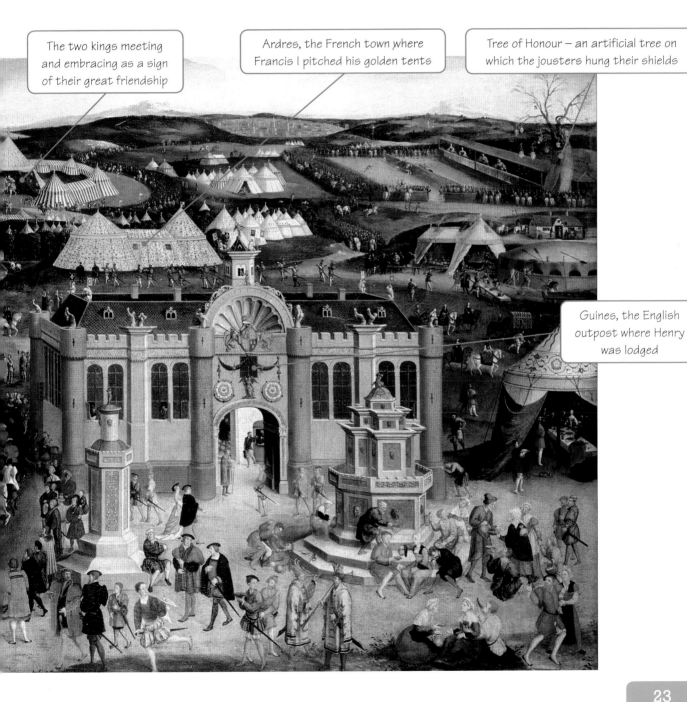

The two kings meeting and embracing as a sign of their great friendship

Ardres, the French town where Francis I pitched his golden tents

Tree of Honour – an artificial tree on which the jousters hung their shields

Guines, the English outpost where Henry was lodged

3.3 Your enquiry: What was Wolsey's greatest achievement, 1515–25?

The Field of Cloth of Gold was a spectacular event, but spectacular events are not always the most important events. The rest of this chapter explores the enquiry question above by looking at the rest of Wolsey's work as Henry's Chief Minister up to 1525.

Your hypothesis

A hypothesis is your first suggested answer to the enquiry question. Having a hypothesis helps you remain focused on the question throughout the enquiry and stops you getting lost in too much information. Later in this book we will ask you to create your own hypotheses but as this is the first enquiry here is a hypothesis to begin with:

Wolsey's greatest achievement was the Field of Cloth of Gold because it made Henry look as powerful as other European rulers.

By the end of the enquiry you will have decided whether the evidence confirms this hypothesis or suggests that a different policy was the greatest achievement.

Collecting evidence to test the hypothesis

Your task is to collect evidence about each of Wolsey's policies. The cards below show you which policies you will be investigating.

Domestic policies

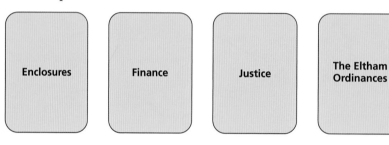

| Enclosures | Finance | Justice | The Eltham Ordinances | The Amicable Grant |

Foreign policies

| The Treaty of London 1518 | The Field of Cloth of Gold 1520 | Foreign policies 1521–25 |

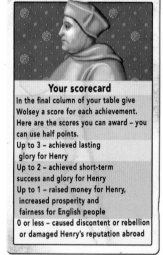

Your scorecard
In the final column of your table give Wolsey a score for each achievement. Here are the scores you can award – you can use half points.
Up to 3 – achieved lasting glory for Henry
Up to 2 – achieved short-term success and glory for Henry
Up to 1 – raised money for Henry, increased prosperity and fairness for English people
0 or less – caused discontent or rebellion or damaged Henry's reputation abroad

Create your own large copy of the table below. Read pages 25–29 and complete the row for each policy in turn. When you reach the final column give each policy a score using the scorecard shown to guide you.

Policy	Wolsey's aims	What did Wolsey do?	Evidence for success	Evidence for failure	Score for achievement
Enclosures					

3.4 Wolsey's domestic policies

Henry VIII was not greatly interested in everyday government, preferring to spend his time on hunting, music, jousting and other enjoyments. He left the hard work of government to Wolsey. Wolsey attempted reforms to make government more efficient, the law fairer or to increase the King's income. However, none of them was completely successful, largely because Wolsey was trying to do so many things at once and domestic plans always had to take second place to King Henry's ambitions for war and diplomacy abroad. Pages 25–26 describe Wolsey's attempts at reforms – and the enemies they created.

ENCLOSURES

The problem: Most villages had large fields shared by villagers as farmland. There were no hedges dividing one person's land from another's. This land was rented by villagers from the local landowner. Villagers also shared rough common land for grazing their animals. However, landowners were increasingly taking over villagers' land because they expected to make more money by keeping sheep on the land and selling the wool than from the rents paid by villagers. Landowners also 'enclosed' the common land with fences for their own use and to keep villagers' animals from grazing on it.

These enclosures gave landowners the chance to try new ideas but caused unemployment. Far fewer workers were needed to look after sheep than to grow crops in the fields. As a result, unemployed labourers moved to towns in search of work and increased the number of 'wandering poor', who were known as vagrants.

Wolsey's actions: Wolsey tried to support common people against landowners. In 1517 he began law cases against 260 landowners for enclosing land illegally. This made him enemies among the landowners who resented his interference.

Results: Wolsey did not reduce the number of enclosures because landowners were not just being greedy. They were struggling for money themselves and so continued to enclose land, and so unemployment increased.

FINANCE

The problem: The king had two kinds of income:

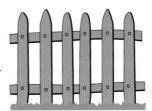

1. Ordinary income – mostly money from rents paid by people who farmed land owned by the King. This income was expected to pay the costs of the King and his family but not for special events such as wars.
2. Extraordinary income – taxes voted by Parliament, usually to pay for wars. These taxes were called tenths and fifteenths because in theory townspeople paid one-tenth of the value of their belongings and country people paid one-fifteenth. However, these taxes had become fixed amounts and were not based on accurate assessments of people's wealth. This was unfair and unpopular – and did not raise enough money for war.

Wolsey's actions: Wolsey tried to increase the King's income from rents by passing an Act of Parliament in 1515, which took back lands given away by Henry since 1509. Second, he replaced the fifteenth and tenth tax with a new tax called a subsidy, based on the real wealth of taxpayers.

Results: The crown did collect more money from the subsidy. However, royal spending continued to be greater than income. Wolsey raised over £800,000 for the King between 1509 and 1520 but government expenditure was £1,700,000, over twice as much because of the costs of warfare. This forced the crown to sell more land and so its ordinary income from rents fell even further.

JUSTICE

The problem: It was difficult for the poor to take legal cases to court because of the high costs and so they were far more likely to suffer bad treatment or be cheated. There was also a lot of corruption in courts such as the rich intimidating or bribing juries to make decisions in their favour.

Wolsey's actions: Wolsey wanted everyone to get fair treatment in the courts. In 1516 he made reforms aiming to punish corruption, especially to stop the rich buying the results they wanted in court. For example, the Earl of Northumberland was imprisoned for refusing to obey a court's decision. Wolsey also acted as a judge himself several times a week in the Court of Star Chamber and set up a court just to deal with cases brought by poor people.

Results: Some people were helped, but far more poor people wanted to use the courts than the courts could deal with, so many were still dissatisfied. Wolsey did not have enough time to deal with this problem because of the time he had to spend dealing with foreign policy. He also gained more enemies among the wealthy who were punished by the courts.

THE ELTHAM ORDINANCES

The problem: The Royal Household contained the royal family, their friends and all the servants who kept the Household fed, clothed and entertained. The cost of the Household was very high as, for example, 500 meals were needed twice a day. In addition, a group of young noblemen in the Household were trying to persuade the King to reduce Wolsey's power.

Wolsey's actions: In 1519, and again in 1526, he made a plan at Eltham Palace proposing changes known as the Eltham Ordinances. These changes would have saved money by cutting down the number of courtiers (whom he called 'rascals and vagabonds') in the Household and, in turn, this would have stopped his political rivals having direct access to the King.

Results: No changes were ever made, partly because Wolsey had to spend his time trying to get the King's marriage annulled. He may also have decided he could find more effective ways to reduce the nobles' influence with the King. As a result no money was saved.

THE AMICABLE GRANT

The problem: In 1525 Henry wanted to invade France to take advantage of King Francis being held prisoner by Emperor Charles V. Wolsey tried to raise money for the war but Parliament refused to agree to a new tax because:

- Wolsey had made people pay a Forced Loan in 1522 but the money lent to the King had still not been repaid.
- Parliament had agreed to a tax in 1523 but that money was still being collected, so why was another tax needed?

Wolsey's actions: Wolsey decided to collect another tax without first asking Parliament. Wolsey claimed this would be simply a friendly or amicable gift of money, given out of the goodness of the people's hearts and their love for King Henry. This tax is therefore known as the Amicable Grant.

The results: The tax was deeply unpopular. In some areas there was high unemployment and rising prices so people could not afford to pay. There was widespread resistance to paying and protests from the Church about paying the tax. In East Anglia there was a rebellion (known as the Amicable Grant Rising). Reports said that 4000 rebels gathered at Lavenham in Suffolk to march to London in protest. The Duke of Suffolk was sent to end the protest but the rebels outnumbered his forces. Suffolk told Wolsey that his troops sympathised with the rebels and 'against their neighbours they would not fight'. As a result of so much hostility Wolsey had to abandon the grant and pardon the leaders of the rebellion. In addition, Henry abandoned his planned invasion of France.

3.5 Wolsey's foreign policy

Wolsey's aims in foreign policy were not exactly the same as Henry's! Henry preferred war. In contrast, Wolsey knew that war was both risky and expensive so unless there was a very high chance of success in war, he preferred peace. The two men agreed, however, that England's ultimate aim was to be seen as the equal to the two most powerful states – France and the Holy Roman Empire. To achieve this, England would have to 'punch above its weight', both in diplomacy and in war. Wolsey's problem was convincing Henry that he could win just as much glory and recognition as a powerful ruler through diplomacy as he could by fighting battles.

Some historians also used to say that Wolsey had one other aim, to be elected as Pope. Popes were (and still are) chosen by the College of Cardinals in Rome, and since Wolsey was a cardinal, he was eligible. However, it was three hundred years since an Englishman had been Pope, and Wolsey knew very well that the cardinals in Italy had the most votes and were certain to choose an Italian cardinal as Pope. Therefore, it is highly unlikely that Wolsey ever thought he had a chance of becoming Pope.

Three rivals – England, France and the Holy Roman Empire

The rivalry in Europe was not just rivalry over the power of the countries – for Henry it was much more personal than that. He was very aware of King Francis of France and Emperor Charles V as personal rivals. He did not want to play 'third fiddle' to Francis and Charles when he was slightly older than them and had become king before they had. Henry very much wanted to be seen as their superior. When he met an Italian ambassador who had seen Francis, Henry wanted to know if Francis was as tall as he was, if Francis was as well-built and whether Francis had such strong and shapely legs. (On page 29 you will have the chance to sum up England's relationships with these rivals after you have looked at the individual events.)

▲ Charles V, the Holy Roman Emperor

Born 1500 – aged 19 in 1519

1506 – Ruler of Burgundy and Netherlands

1516 – King of Spain

1519 – Holy Roman Emperor

▲ Francis I, King of France

Born 1494 – aged 25 in 1519

1515 – King of France

▲ Henry VIII of England

Born 1491 – aged 28 in 1519

1509 – King of England

The Treaty of London, 1518

As you read on page 18, Henry had already invaded France in 1513. This had been a very expensive expedition, which had achieved nothing, but Henry felt successful because he had won the skirmish called 'the Battle of the Spurs'. His desire for war increased further when Francis I became King of France, but Henry could not find allies to fight France.

Francis I had a very different aim – to invade and take land in northern Italy. When the Pope appealed to Henry for help against Francis, Henry declared pompously and optimistically: 'If I choose, Francis will cross the Alps [into Italy] and if I choose he will not.'

Henry completely exaggerated his own power. He did not have the military strength or wealth to stop Francis. Wolsey worked hard to win allies to fight France but failed. Nobody wanted to risk losing a war against France. By 1515, Francis had successfully invaded Italy, won a major battle and taken land – everything Henry had hoped to do, but had not. Henry and England were helpless on the sidelines while his rival, Francis, won all the glory.

Then, in 1518, the situation changed – thanks to the Turks! A Muslim army from Turkey attacked Italy and the Pope appealed to the Christian rulers of Europe for help. Wolsey pounced on the idea and hijacked it. He called a large meeting in London, inviting all the rulers of Europe to send ambassadors. They did – and they agreed a treaty of 'universal peace' called the Treaty of London as a prelude to helping the Pope. Part of this bigger Treaty was a peace agreement between England and France, which also arranged the marriage of Henry's baby daughter, Mary, to the son of Francis I.

The Treaty of London said that all the countries of Europe would live at peace with each other. If anyone broke the peace the other countries would punish the treaty-breaker. At the time the Treaty was called a moral and diplomatic triumph.

Most importantly for Henry it had taken place in London and he had been at the centre of events. Henry looked like the man who had united the whole of Europe in peace. Wolsey had done the work, but the glory was Henry's.

The Field of Cloth of Gold, 1520

Between 1518 and 1520 Wolsey tried to uphold Henry's reputation as the peacemaker of Europe, created by the Treaty of London. To do this he organised two great conferences between Henry and Charles V, and two more between Henry and Francis – one of which was the Field of Cloth of Gold. Henry did his part, even turning down an invitation from Charles to ally together in a war against France.

The Field of Cloth of Gold symbolised Wolsey's success in keeping Henry at the centre of events. He made Henry look like one of the three great rulers of Europe – a great achievement. However, decisions made elsewhere ended this success as a major war was about to begin between France and the Holy Roman Empire.

The Field of Cloth of Gold had been a great moment for Henry and Wolsey. They had looked like men who were controlling events in Europe. Wolsey had done as much as anyone could have done to make Henry appear a great king. However, once Francis and Charles decided to go to war against each other there was nothing Henry and Wolsey could do to stop them.

Henry and Wolsey faced a choice – should they stay out of the war and sit on the sidelines, or join the war by allying with either Charles V or Francis I? Staying on the sidelines was impossible. It made England – and Henry – look powerless. They chose Charles as their ally because it was natural to go to war against France, England's traditional enemy.

Foreign policies, 1521–25

In 1521 Henry made a treaty with Charles and, the next year, England declared war on France. Henry must have hoped that, with Charles as his ally, he was about to win the military glory he had wanted all along. However, Wolsey still hoped to avoid the risk and expense of war and continued peace negotiations with France.

This disagreement about foreign policy between Henry and Wolsey was bad enough, but what led to the failures of the next few years was the failure of Henry and Charles to support each other. Charles was chiefly interested in defeating the French army in northern Italy – he was not interested in invading France. In contrast, Henry was only interested in invading France. The result was that the alliance between Henry and Charles never achieved anything.

In 1523 an English army led by the Duke of Suffolk invaded France. As there was a rebellion taking place in France the English got within 50 miles of Paris, but the expected support from Charles's army did not arrive. Henry decided against joining his army and the English turned and went home. The brief promise of success had turned into another expensive failure.

Then came the Battle of Pavia in northern Italy in 1525. Charles's army destroyed the French and captured King Francis. When the news arrived in London, Henry rejoiced and made plans to invade and conquer France. He expected that he and Charles would divide France between them – but Charles did not want France. He wanted to control northern Italy and had already got what he wanted. Besides, Charles did not think that England had given him any real help in four years of war, so why should he now help England?

Henry's hope of invading France finally ended when the Amicable Grant Rising broke out in England (see page 26) and he could not raise money for war. His hopes of glory were over. Instead, Wolsey negotiated a peace treaty with France and abandoned the alliance with Charles – a decision that would come back to haunt Henry and Wolsey a few short years later.

ENGLAND, FRANCE AND THE HOLY ROMAN EMPIRE

Now you have completed your work on Wolsey's foreign policy to 1525 this activity sums up English relations with France and the Holy Roman Empire.

The middle line in the chart below shows England's policy. It shows England being neutral from 1515 to 1521. Your tasks are:

1. Draw your own copy of the chart. Look at the line showing England's policy 1515–21. Decide if it accurately shows English policy. If it does, add annotations that provide evidence to show that England was neutral. If you disagree, draw your own line and add annotations to justify your drawing.

2. Complete the line for 1521 to 1525, adding annotations to justify how you have drawn the line.

3. a) Explain the pattern of England's relations with France in the period 1515–1525.
   b) Explain the pattern of England's relations with the Holy Roman Empire in this period.

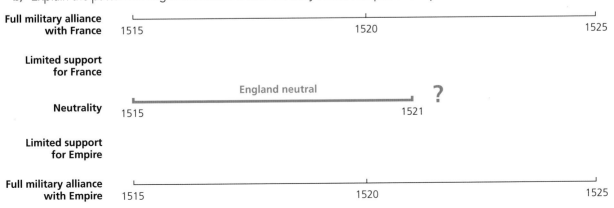

29

3.6 Communicating your answer

Your enquiry has been exploring Wolsey's policies and which of them was his greatest achievement. If this topic appeared in an exam the question might look like this:

'Wolsey's greatest success between 1515 and 1525 was the Field of Cloth of Gold.' How far do you agree? Explain your answer.

Now you have completed your research it's time to write your answer …

STOP! We have forgotten something very important:

Revise your hypothesis and get your summary answer clear in your mind before you start to write.

STOP

It's time to THINK about the answer

This is a really vital stage because one of the biggest mistakes that students make is starting to write their answer without having the answer clear in their minds. These activities help you do that and they will work better if you discuss them with a partner.

1. Look at the scores in the final column of your completed table from page 24. Now you have completed all your research do you agree that the policy with the highest score was Wolsey's greatest success? Identify two reasons to support your judgement.
2. Use your completed table to write a paragraph answering the question. Include one or two other policies which you think were successes as well as Wolsey's greatest success. This paragraph provides a clear answer to the question.

Now it's time to write your answer.

You will find more guidance on answering this type of question on page 116 and you can use the Word Wall shown here to assist you. However, the person who will give you the best advice is your teacher because he or she knows exactly what help you need to improve your work in History.

The Word Wall – language is power!

Building your own Word Wall such as the one below, maybe on a piece of A3 paper, helps you to:

a) understand the meaning of words, phrases and names that relate to life in the sixteenth century
b) communicate clearly and precisely when you describe or explain historical events. This definitely helps you do well in your exams
c) spell these important words correctly. Marks are lost in exams for poor spelling.

You give yourself the best chance of doing well in your exams if you take responsibility for your own learning. You need to identify words:

- whose meaning you are not sure of
- you can't spell correctly every time.

1. Make sure you find out their meaning and spelling and which topics they are linked to.
2. Add to your Word Wall all the words you will need from Chapters 1, 2 and 3. Looking back at these chapters now is a good reminder of what you covered.

foreign policy   domestic

policy   alliance   treaty

forced loan   enclosures   subsidy

administration   vagrants   negotiator

skirmish   justice   corruption

intimidation   chaplain   diplomacy

Battle of the Spurs   Field of Cloth of Gold

Treaty of London   Amicable Grant

Court of Star Chamber

Eltham Ordinances

Practice questions

1. Describe two features of:
   a) Wolsey's rise to power
   b) The Treaty of London (1518)
   c) The Amicable Grant (1525)
2. Explain why Wolsey's foreign policy did not win military glory for Henry VIII.
3. Explain why Wolsey's domestic reforms were not as successful as he wished.
4. 'Wolsey's desire for peace was the main reason why Henry VIII did not achieve military success 1515–25.' How far do you agree? Explain your answer.

Some of your exam questions will suggest two topics you could use in your answer. You can see examples on page 112.

We have not included topics in the practice questions in this book to give teachers the opportunity to change the topics with questions from year to year.

Remember that questions as well as topics change every year.

3.7 Visible learning – developing independence

On page 8 we introduced the idea of making learning **visible** – if you can see and describe how you go about learning you will learn more effectively. This page is a crucial example of visible learning. What you see below is your route-map – how to get from knowing a **little** about a topic to knowing a **lot** about it. It is important because in the future you will need the skills to study independently, perhaps at A level, university or at work. The route-map or process below will help you work independently and effectively. The box below shows the process in six stages; the diagram then explains it more fully.

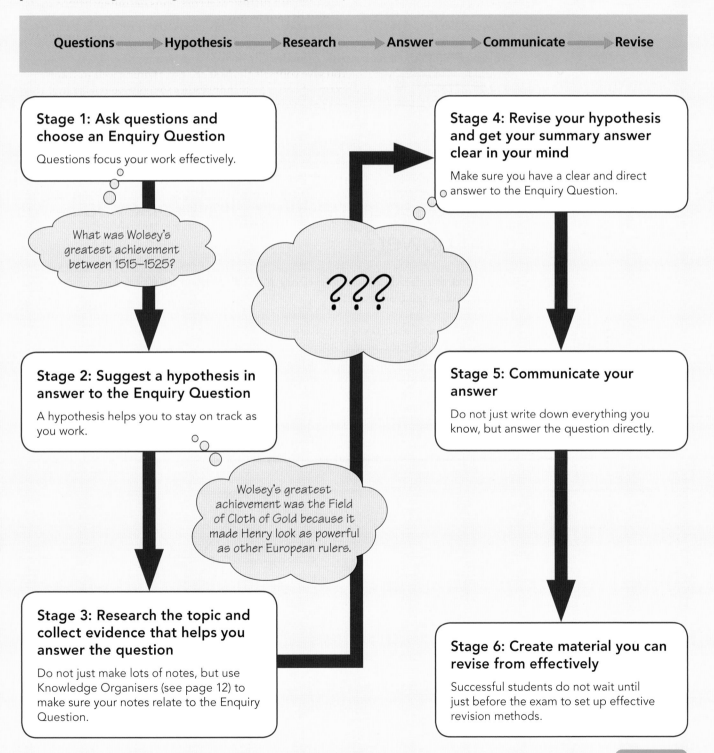

Questions ➡ Hypothesis ➡ Research ➡ Answer ➡ Communicate ➡ Revise

Stage 1: Ask questions and choose an Enquiry Question

Questions focus your work effectively.

What was Wolsey's greatest achievement between 1515–1525?

Stage 2: Suggest a hypothesis in answer to the Enquiry Question

A hypothesis helps you to stay on track as you work.

Wolsey's greatest achievement was the Field of Cloth of Gold because it made Henry look as powerful as other European rulers.

Stage 3: Research the topic and collect evidence that helps you answer the question

Do not just make lots of notes, but use Knowledge Organisers (see page 12) to make sure your notes relate to the Enquiry Question.

Stage 4: Revise your hypothesis and get your summary answer clear in your mind

Make sure you have a clear and direct answer to the Enquiry Question.

Stage 5: Communicate your answer

Do not just write down everything you know, but answer the question directly.

Stage 6: Create material you can revise from effectively

Successful students do not wait until just before the exam to set up effective revision methods.

4 The downfall of Wolsey, 1525–29

Cardinal Wolsey died at Leicester Abbey in November 1530. He was travelling south from York to London to stand trial for treason where he would, in all likelihood, have been found guilty and then executed. He must have dreaded the public humiliation and the gloating of the nobility as they watched the butcher's son from Ipswich cut down to size.

However, Wolsey's downfall was not sudden. He lost his power and positions late in 1529, but it was another year before he was charged with treason. During this year Wolsey's feelings must have swung from despair to hope and back to despair. At times he still received messages from Henry to 'be of good cheer'. Was Henry about to forgive Wolsey and bring him back into power? It seemed that, for many months, Henry could not decide whether to save or break the cardinal – but, in the end, he broke him.

4.1 Your enquiry: Why did Wolsey fall from power?

1. Use what you already know about Henry and Wolsey. Make a list of the reasons why you think Wolsey fell from power.
2. Use the time-chart on page 33. Select the four most important steps in Wolsey's fall from power and write them on your own copy of the steps shown here, working up the steps in chronological order. Underneath, explain the significance of each step.
3. What evidence on page 33 supports the reasons in your list?
4. What new reasons can you find to explain Wolsey's fall?
5. Make a copy of the mind map below. Pencil your reasons for Wolsey's fall into the boxes.
6. Write a paragraph summing up your thoughts about why Wolsey fell from power. This is your hypothesis (see page 31). Use one or more of these phrases:

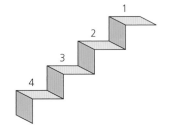

Reasons, causes and factors

Reasons, causes and factors all mean the same thing. We have mostly used the word 'reason' in this chapter but do not be puzzled if the reasons are sometimes referred to as 'causes' or 'factors'.

key reason for	contributed to	a significant reason	played an important role

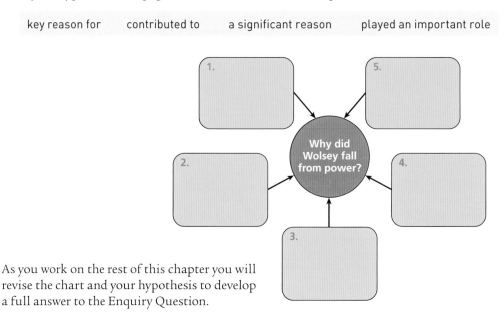

As you work on the rest of this chapter you will revise the chart and your hypothesis to develop a full answer to the Enquiry Question.

The choir singing anthems during the funeral

Monks carrying Wolsey's coffin in the funeral procession

Wolsey's coffin lying in the abbey

▲ This picture shows the funeral of Cardinal Wolsey at Leicester Abbey. It is taken from *Thomas Wolsey, late Cardinal, his Life and Death*, written by George Cavendish in the 1550s. Cavendish served Wolsey as a close personal attendant from 1522 to 1530.

THE ROAD TO WOLSEY'S FALL

1527: Henry instructed Wolsey to approach Pope Clement VII to annul his marriage to Catherine of Aragon.

October 1528: The Pope sent Cardinal Campeggio to England to lead a Commission to decide whether Henry's marriage to Catherine should be annulled.

June 1529: Wolsey joined Campeggio to head the Commission to decide on the divorce proceedings. It looked as if the case would be decided in England, where it was likely to go in Henry's favour.

June 1529: Emperor Charles V defeated the French army at the Battle of Landriano. Charles had been in control of Rome and the Pope since 1527, and now he dominated Europe as a whole.

July 1529: The Pope recalled the annulment case to Rome, so the case would not be decided in England and therefore Henry would probably not get the annulment. A group of nobles tried and failed to bring about Wolsey's downfall.

A family link

Charles V was related to Catherine of Aragon. Charles was Catherine's nephew.

September 1529: Wolsey was suspended from his Archdiocese at York, and stripped of his palaces at Winchester and St Albans. But he also received a jewelled ring and a note from Henry telling him to 'be of good cheer'.

October 1529: Wolsey was charged with *praemunire*, the crime of serving a foreign power (the Pope in this case) instead of the King. Wolsey's greatest public office, the Chancellorship, was taken from him and given to Sir Thomas More.

February 1530: Wolsey received a royal pardon and was allowed again to take up his duties as the Archbishop of York.

April 1530: Wolsey was ordered to move to York, away from London and the Court. In desperation, Wolsey began writing to Francis I, Charles V, the Pope and Catherine of Aragon to try to broker a deal that might restore Henry's faith in him.

November 1530: Wolsey was arrested, charged with treason and ordered to return to London to face trial. On the journey south, at Leicester, Wolsey died.

4.2 Catherine of Aragon, Anne Boleyn and the succession

One reason you probably included in your explanation of Wolsey's fall is Henry's wish to end his marriage to Catherine of Aragon. Before we look at exactly how this contributed to Wolsey's fall, we need to tell the story of Henry's marriage and why he wanted to annul it.

Henry and Catherine

Catherine of Aragon was the daughter of the King and Queen of Spain. In 1501, aged 16, she married Arthur, the 15-year-old eldest son of Henry VII. Their marriage sealed an alliance between England and Spain. Six months after the wedding Arthur fell ill and died. Catherine remained in England and in 1509 she married Arthur's brother, Henry VIII, shortly after he became king. This marriage maintained the Spanish alliance.

Before Henry married Catherine, he had to apply for a dispensation (permission) for the marriage from the Pope, Julius II. This was because the Church forbade a man to marry his brother's wife. However, Catherine testified that she had not had intercourse with Arthur before his death, so the dispensation was granted on the grounds that Catherine and Arthur had not consummated their marriage.

▲ A portrait of the young Catherine of Aragon.

The succession – the need for an heir

At first the marriage worked well. Catherine enjoyed life at Court and Henry publically showed his devotion to her. Catherine conceived at least six times before 1518, but only one child survived – Mary, born in 1516. This obviously left Henry without a male heir. As they grew older, Catherine's age began to count against her having a son. Henry stopped sleeping with Catherine in 1524, when she was 39 years old.

The failure to produce a son was interpreted, however unfairly, as Catherine's fault – she had failed to do her duty to the King by not having a healthy son. Worse still, Henry became convinced that the marriage was against Christian law, and that the Pope should not have granted a dispensation for the marriage. Henry saw the deaths of their two baby sons as a punishment from God because he had married his brother's wife. He was also influenced by a passage in the Bible which says:

> And if a man take his brother's wife, it is an unclean thing: he hath uncovered his brother's nakedness [dishonoured his brother]; they shall be childless. (Leviticus 20:21)

In addition, a new translation of the Bible emphasised that such a couple would be denied sons. This confirmed Henry's fear that he was being punished for his marriage to Catherine. If God approved of the marriage, then they would have had healthy sons.

It appears that Henry believed the only way to cleanse his soul and put things right was to end his marriage to Catherine. In 1527 Henry instructed Wolsey to approach Pope Clement VII to annul the marriage, on the grounds that the dispensation granted in 1509 was invalid.

Henry and Anne

By the mid-1520s Henry had fallen in love with Anne Boleyn. Anne had spent her teenage years in the Netherlands and at the Court of Francis I of France, where she was maid of honour to Queen Claude. It is possible that Henry first saw Anne at the Field of Cloth of Gold when he dined with the French queen. In 1522 she returned to England and became maid of honour to Catherine of Aragon. She attracted much attention at Henry VIII's Court and in 1523 was secretly engaged to be married to Henry Percy, son of the Earl of Northumberland. However, by 1526 she had caught the eye of Henry himself, who ordered Wolsey to prevent her marriage to Percy.

Henry had had a number of mistresses during his marriage to Catherine. One of these was Mary Boleyn, Anne's sister. Once Henry fell for Anne, his interest in Mary ended. Unlike her sister, however, Anne Boleyn refused to become Henry's mistress despite Henry's pleading in letters such as this from 1527:

> Henceforth, my heart shall be dedicate to you alone, greatly desirous that so my body could be as well, as God can bring it to pass if it pleaseth Him, whom I entreat once each day for the accomplishment thereof.

Henry had found the woman whom he wanted to be queen, whom he believed would be sure to have sons. All that was now needed was for Wolsey to make sure the Pope annulled Henry's marriage to Catherine. Both Henry and Wolsey must have had great confidence that this would happen, as Popes usually agreed to such requests from kings. Why should this case be any different?

▲ Anne was the daughter of Sir Thomas Boleyn and his wife Lady Elizabeth Howard.

HENRY, CATHERINE AND ANNE

1. Make your own copy of the timeline below. Mark on your timeline the significant events referred to on these pages. Use different colours for events that relate to Catherine and to Anne.

1505	1510	1515	1520	1525	1530

2. How long had Henry been married to Catherine before he began to seek an annulment?
3. Do you think that overall Henry was slow or quick to seek an annulment? Explain your answer.
4. Why was Henry convinced that he needed to end his marriage to Catherine?
5. Why was Henry confident of having the marriage annulled?
6. Given what you have read so far, which of these phrases best describes the importance in Wolsey's fall of Henry's wish for an annulment? Explain your choice.

made it inevitable	created the possibility of	was a major factor in

need not have led to Wolsey's fall at all

? **Visible Learning**

Timelines

Timelines in history books are meant to be useful but they often aren't! This is because we look at them without questions in our minds and so don't really think about the details or pattern of events in the timeline. You will find it easier to understand and remember the sequence of events in the timeline if you draw your own and annotate them with your own notes. This is much more effective than just looking at a timeline in a book.

4.3 Henry's desire to annul his marriage

Henry's quest to have his marriage annulled is sometimes called 'the King's Great Matter' because it dominated Henry's actions and thoughts for several years and was of overwhelming importance to him. Why was it so important to have his marriage annulled by the Pope?

The obvious answer is that the annulment meant he could marry again and have a son, ending fears of war or rebellion over who would be the next king. However, there was more to it than even this important point. Henry's future children would be very important diplomatically as they could be married to foreign princes or princesses to help build alliances with other countries. Other kings would not be interested in marriage alliances with England if:

a) there were doubts whether Henry's marriage to Anne Boleyn was legal, and therefore
b) there were doubts over whether their children were legitimate.

Only a formal, legal annulment of Henry's marriage to Catherine by Pope Clement would get rid of these doubts for the future.

Therefore, the annulment was extremely important. However, Henry's wish for an annulment did not mean that Wolsey's fall was inevitable. If Wolsey had been successful in getting the annulment, his power would have been greater than ever and, at first, in 1527 Henry was confident that Wolsey would succeed. Popes had often annulled marriages before, including that of Henry's sister Margaret.

The Pope's refusal

For two years Henry and Wolsey remained confident. When Cardinal Campeggio arrived in England in 1529 to head an enquiry into the marriage, it looked as if a decision was close and would give Henry what he wanted. Why, then, did Pope Clement refuse to annul Henry's marriage? This diagram summarises the reasons:

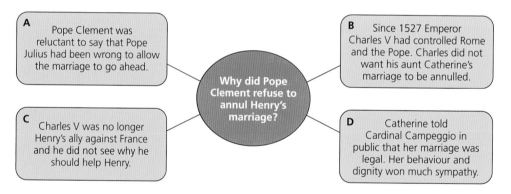

A Pope Clement was reluctant to say that Pope Julius had been wrong to allow the marriage to go ahead.

B Since 1527 Emperor Charles V had controlled Rome and the Pope. Charles did not want his aunt Catherine's marriage to be annulled.

Why did Pope Clement refuse to annul Henry's marriage?

C Charles V was no longer Henry's ally against France and he did not see why he should help Henry.

D Catherine told Cardinal Campeggio in public that her marriage was legal. Her behaviour and dignity won much sympathy.

As a result, Wolsey was powerless to make the Pope change his mind. In July 1529 the Pope recalled the case to Rome, ending the possibility of the marriage being annulled. This decision considerably increased the chances of Wolsey losing power. He had failed to win Henry the annulment he so much desired. Henry was extremely disappointed and angry. This in turn meant that Wolsey's enemies at Court had the chance to persuade Henry to get rid of Wolsey. However, this still did not mean that Wolsey's fall was inevitable.

CATHERINE'S PLEA

In June 1529 Catherine of Aragon appeared before the hearing into the legality of her marriage. Henry VIII was there, and so were many members of the Church and the Court. Catherine's dramatic plea won much sympathy, and included these words directly to Henry:

> Alas! Sir, wherein have I offended you, or what occasion of displeasure have I deserved? I have been to you a true, humble and obedient wife, ever comfortable to your will and pleasure, and that never said or did anything to the contrary thereof, being always well pleased and contented with all things wherein you had any delight or dalliance, whether it were in little or much.... This twenty years or more I have been your true wife and by me ye have had divers children, although it hath pleased God to call them out of this world, which hath been no default in me.

WOLSEY'S FALL – THE ANNULMENT

1. Why was the annulment so important to Henry?

2. Give two reasons why Henry was optimistic about getting the annulment before July 1529.

3. Which reason or reasons in the diagram on page 36 are most likely to explain the Pope's refusal to annul the marriage? Explain your choice of reasons.

4. How would you describe the importance of the failure to have the marriage annulled in Wolsey's fall? You could use one of these phrases or one of your own. Explain your choice.

   made it inevitable

   created the possibility of

   was a major factor in

   need not have led to Wolsey's fall at all

5. Complete one section of your chart from page 32 by:
   a) filling in Box 1 with a reason for Wolsey's fall
   b) writing notes on the arrow explaining how the reason was linked to Wolsey's fall.

   We have modelled how to do this below. You could copy this if you think it is correct but it does need completing!

   c) Revise the hypothesis you wrote on page 32 if your ideas about Wolsey's fall have changed.

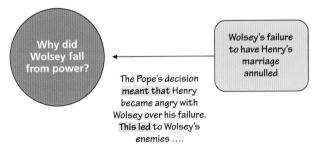

Why did Wolsey fall from power?

The Pope's decision meant that Henry became angry with Wolsey over his failure. This led to Wolsey's enemies ....

Wolsey's failure to have Henry's marriage annulled

Visible learning

'This meant that...': using connectives to tie in what you know to the question

WHAT YOU KNOW — WHAT THE QUESTION ASKS

When talking or writing about the reasons for an event such as Wolsey's fall you cannot just say that a reason led to his fall. You have to prove that the reason led to his fall. You can do this effectively by using **golden words and phrases** such as 'this meant that…', 'this led to…' and 'this resulted in…'.

We call these words and phrases **connectives** because they connect what you know to the question and prove they are strongly linked. Connectives will help you write a good answer to the Enquiry Question.

4.4 Foreign policy failures

The diagram on page 36 said that Charles V 'did not see why he should help Henry'. This may partly have been because Catherine of Aragon was Charles's aunt and he did not want to see his aunt humiliated, which could also have damaged his own reputation. However, Charles's anger at English foreign policy probably played a bigger part in his decision to oppose the annulment. There were two reasons for this:

1. In 1521 Henry and Charles had signed a treaty, promising to go to war together against France (see page 29). Henry did eventually invade France in 1523, but by then it was too late. Charles felt that Henry had failed to help him against France. Therefore, when England wanted to invade France again in 1525, Charles refused to help.

2. After 1525 Charles's Empire dominated Europe. In 1527 Wolsey arranged a peace treaty between England and France and then England declared war on the Holy Roman Empire in 1528. Therefore, England had become Charles's enemy, when Wolsey needed Charles's support to get Henry's marriage annulled. This is summarised in the diagram below.

1. Charles took control of Rome and the Pope in 1527.	2. Henry and Wolsey needed Charles's support to persuade the Pope to annul the marriage.	**BUT**	3. England had not supported Charles's war with France and later went to war with Charles's Empire.	**SO**	4. Charles did not help Henry and Wolsey as they had not helped him against France.

As Wolsey had been the leading figure in English foreign policy since 1525, he took the blame for the past failure to support Charles now rebounding and preventing Henry getting the annulment.

WOLSEY'S FALL – FOREIGN POLICY FAILURES

1. Explain why Charles V refused to support Henry's wish for an annulment.
2. Complete Box 2 in your chart from page 32. Use connectives to explain the links to Wolsey's fall.
3. How would you describe the importance of foreign policy failures in Wolsey's fall? Explain your choice of phrase.
4. Revise the hypothesis you wrote on page 32 if your ideas about Wolsey's fall have changed.

4.5 Wolsey's background and personality

Hardly anyone supported Wolsey once he was blamed for the failure to get the annulment. This can be explained by Wolsey's background and personality and how he appeared to enjoy monopolising power at others' expense. Wolsey certainly enjoyed showing off his wealth. A description by George Cavendish, one of his servants, recounts how Wolsey travelled:

> with two great crosses of silver carried before him, with his sergeant-at-arms carrying a silver mace and with his ushers shouting out 'My lords and masters, make way for the Lord's Grace.'

Kings and nobles were expected to show off their wealth, but it was easy to criticise a butcher's son who seemed to enjoy showing how powerful he was compared to dukes and earls. However clever he was, Wolsey was the son of a butcher (see page 18) and his rise to be Henry's Chief Minister and a cardinal was unusual in a period when kings were expected to take advice from noblemen. Therefore, some nobles resented Wolsey and felt that they had been pushed aside by him. However, they had been able to do little while Wolsey was successful and the King had confidence in him.

Wolsey's failure to win the King the annulment changed that situation. Now Wolsey was vulnerable to enemies who could blacken his reputation with the King. In the summer of 1529 Henry was given a book containing over thirty accusations against Wolsey. At the head of the accusers were the Dukes of Norfolk and Suffolk, the two most powerful noblemen in the country.

Despite this, Henry did not yet dismiss Wolsey or accuse him of treason. Look back at the time-chart showing the road to Wolsey's fall on page 33 and you will see that he held on to power until the autumn of 1529. His background and personality had made him enemies, and the enemies were trying to bring him down, but this again did not make his fall inevitable.

▲ Two of Wolsey's major enemies, the Dukes of Norfolk (left) and Suffolk (right). Thomas Howard, Duke of Norfolk, was one of the commanders who beat the Scots at Flodden and was the uncle of Anne Boleyn. Charles Brandon, Duke of Suffolk, was Henry's friend and jousting companion. He married Henry's sister, Mary, after her first husband, the King of France, died – although Henry was far from pleased about this as he wanted Mary to make another **diplomatic marriage** abroad. In 1529 Brandon declared in public 'the old saying is true, no Cardinal ever did any good in England'.

WOLSEY'S FALL – HIS BACKGROUND AND PERSONALITY

1. Explain why nobles resented Wolsey's position as Chief Minister.
2. Complete Box 3 in your chart from page 32. Use connectives to explain the links to Wolsey's fall.
3. How would you describe the importance of Wolsey's background and personality in his fall? Explain your choice of phrase.
4. Revise the hypothesis you wrote on page 32 if your ideas about Wolsey's fall have changed.

4.6 The Boleyn faction

A faction was a group of nobles who worked together to influence the King or competed with other factions to influence the King and increase their own power. A faction often formed around one powerful individual and often wanted to see the King follow a particular policy such as war against France.

The Boleyn faction developed around Anne Boleyn in the late 1520s and, in 1529, it played a large part in Wolsey's fall. The key members of this faction are shown on the left:

Anne was at the centre of the Boleyn faction because, as Cardinal Campeggio noted early in 1529, Henry's love for Anne was:

> something amazing, and in fact he sees nothing and thinks nothing but Anne. He cannot stay away from her for an hour.

Henry's love meant that Anne was the person with by far the greatest influence on King Henry. She was supported by the great power and experience of her uncle, the Duke of Norfolk.

It was no accident that there was a Boleyn faction at Henry's Court. Both sisters, Mary and Anne, were placed at Court by their family to develop stronger links with the King and, hopefully, increase the family's influence, wealth and honours. While Mary was Henry's mistress her father was made a Knight of the Garter and then Viscount Rochford in 1525. Anne's influence led to further honours in 1529, as you can see in the diagram on the left.

Anne Boleyn and Wolsey

Cardinal Campeggio closed the divorce proceedings at the Conference in London in July 1529. By then Anne clearly blamed Wolsey for the failure to get the annulment. To Anne, Wolsey was an obstacle to her marrying Henry. Anne's influence over Henry was probably crucial in the first stage of Wolsey's fall in October 1529 when he was dismissed as Chancellor and ceased to be the King's Chief Minister. Norfolk and Suffolk replaced him as Henry's chief councillors.

Even so, Wolsey still hoped to return to power and for several months Wolsey's fate hung in the balance. At times it appeared that Henry might recall Wolsey, and the Boleyns feared that if he returned to power he would take his revenge on them. Therefore they, and particularly Anne, continued to tell Henry that Wolsey should be put on trial, perhaps for treason. Everything depended on how Henry felt about Wolsey.

▲ Opposing factions around the King could lead to violence.

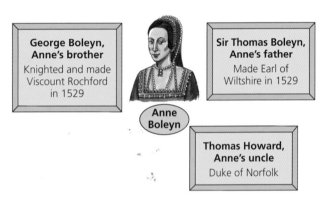

George Boleyn, Anne's brother Knighted and made Viscount Rochford in 1529

Anne Boleyn

Sir Thomas Boleyn, Anne's father Made Earl of Wiltshire in 1529

Thomas Howard, Anne's uncle Duke of Norfolk

KEY DATES – A REMINDER

July 1529: Cardinal Campeggio ended the proceedings in London about the annulment. The case was to be dealt with in Rome.

October 1529: The first stage of Wolsey's fall – he lost his roles as Chancellor and Chief Minister.

November 1530: The second stage of Wolsey's fall – he was charged with treason and ordered to return to London for trial.

WOLSEY'S FALL – THE BOLEYN FACTION ?

1. Who were the key members of the Boleyn faction?
2. Why did the Boleyn faction have so much influence over Henry?
3. Complete Box 4 in your chart from page 32. Use connectives to explain the links to Wolsey's fall.
4. How would you describe the importance of the Boleyn faction in Wolsey's fall? Explain your choice of phrase.
5. Revise the hypothesis you wrote on page 32 if your ideas about Wolsey's fall have changed.

4.7 Henry's decision

When discussing any event in the sixteenth century it is vital to remember that the King or queen took all the major decisions, about going to war or whom his or her chief advisers were. No one else could take these decisions, even if many people tried to influence them. Henry VIII, however, was never good at taking major decisions – he often hesitated, unable to make his mind up.

Henry's attitude to Wolsey is a good example of his indecisiveness. Although he dismissed Wolsey from key posts in 1529 and at times was deeply angry with him, at other times he sent him messages to be of good cheer, implying Wolsey might well return as Chief Minister. He even said on one occasion that 'in managing business Wolsey was a better man than any of them', meaning his new advisers. This must have alarmed the Boleyns greatly.

In the end, Wolsey's enemies found the evidence they needed to push Henry into making the decision they wanted. They reported to Henry that Wolsey had been writing letters to the Emperor Charles, to the King of France and to the Pope, supposedly to win their support for ending the relationship between Henry and Anne. The King of France also said that he had received letters from Wolsey.

We do not know if Wolsey really wrote these letters, but the evidence given to Henry convinced him that Wolsey had betrayed him. It seemed that Wolsey had put his loyalty to the Pope and to Queen Catherine before his loyalty to Henry – and there was nothing Henry hated more than disloyalty.

These charges led directly to Henry ordering Wolsey's arrest and trial for treason. Wolsey now lost all hope of returning to power, saying:

> I see how the matter against me is framed, but if I had served my God as diligently as I have done the King he would not have given me over in my grey hairs.

However, Wolsey cheated the enemies who hoped to see him humiliated at his trial. He died, as you read on page 33, on his way south, at Leicester.

WOLSEY'S FALL – HENRY'S DECISION ?

1. Why was Henry's attitude to Wolsey such an important influence on his fate?
2. What led to Wolsey being accused of treason?
3. Why did this evidence have such a powerful impact on Henry?
4. What do you think Wolsey meant in the quotation 'I see how the matter … is framed…' above?
5. Complete Box 5 in your chart from page 32. Use connectives to explain the links to Wolsey's fall.

◄ This portrait of Henry VIII by Joos van Cleve was painted in the early 1530s.

4.8 Concluding your enquiry: Why did Wolsey fall from power?

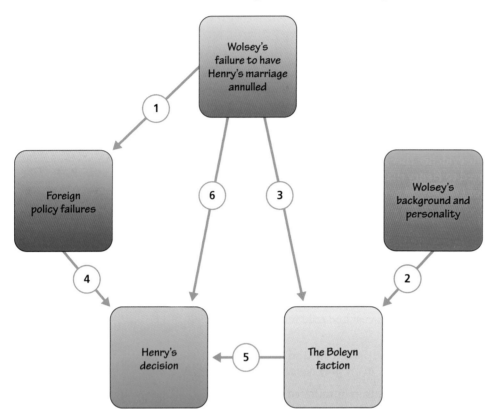

Linking the causes of Wolsey's fall

You have been exploring how each cause or reason helps to explain Wolsey's fall from power. Now you can use the knowledge you have built up to identify how the causes were linked.

The lines in this diagram show which reasons were inter-linked. Your task is to write at least one sentence explaining each of the six links. You can find the explanations on pages 36–41, but first try to do this task without looking back to see how much you can remember.

The best way to do this is to draw your own version of the diagram on a large piece of paper and to write your explanations on to your diagram.

Prioritising the reasons – mind your language!

Throughout this chapter we have been asking you to think about the phrases or words you would use to describe the significance of each reason in Wolsey's fall. You always need to be careful with the language you use when you write about different reasons or causes. Select words and phrases very carefully – aim to be as precise as possible – so that your argument about which reasons are most important is very clear to your reader.

Use the Word Wall below to decide how you would describe the role of each reason in Wolsey's fall.

If you want to show that a factor was the most important cause:	If you want to show that a cause was very important:	If you want to show a cause was important:
...was the essential reason why...	A crucial reason why ... was...	...also played an important role in...
...was the main cause of...	...played a major role in...	
The key reason for ... was...	...was a significant reason for...	...influenced...
The most influential reason for ... was...	...was also highly important in...	...contributed to... ...also determined why...

Communicating your answer

At the beginning of this chapter on page 32 we asked you to think about what you knew to begin with and to write a hypothesis giving your first thoughts on the reasons for Wolsey's fall from power. Now you have studied the topic in detail you have enough information and understanding of the reasons for Wolsey's fall to enable you to answer confidently and effectively this examination-style question:

Explain why Wolsey fell from power in 1529.

On pages 116–17 you will find detailed guidance for answering this kind of 'explain' question. However, before you look at those pages, think back to your work so far:

1. Work with a partner and use your answers from the activities on page 42 to discuss and identify which reasons were most significant in Wolsey's fall from power.
2. Write a short paragraph summarising your answer to the question, making sure you identify those main reasons. This makes sure you have the answer clear in your mind before you begin writing.
3. Plan in what sequence you will cover the main reasons in your answer.
4. For each reason identify one or two pieces of information that justify your statement that a reason led to the dispute. In other words:

Don't just say a reason caused Wolsey to fall from power – PROVE it.

To do this, use your connective phrases such as 'this led to' and 'this resulted in'.

Now read pages 116–17 and then you can write a good answer!

Visible learning

How does talking help?

Some people think that students are only working effectively if the classroom is quiet. This is wrong. Experience shows that students write better answers if they have first talked through their answer with other people. Talking helps us organise ideas in our minds, choose the right words and decide what evidence we need to prove a point.

Updating your Word Wall

These words – along with the words in the Word Wall opposite – will help you answer questions on this topic in your exam. Therefore you need to understand all of them – can you explain why each of them could be useful?

dispensation   annulment

praemunire   faction

consummated   invalid

monopolise   diplomatic marriage

Campeggio   Clement VII

King's Great Matter

This meant that... This led to...
This resulted in...

Practice questions

1. Describe two features of:
   a) Henry's marriage to Catherine of Aragon
   b) The opposition to the annulment
   c) The Boleyn faction.
2. Explain why Henry VIII failed to gain an annulment of his marriage to Catherine of Aragon.
3. 'The opposition of the Emperor Charles V was the main reason why Henry VIII failed to gain an annulment of his marriage to Catherine of Aragon.' How far do you agree? Explain your answer.
4. 'Wolsey's failure to gain an annulment of Henry's marriage was the main reason why he fell from power in 1529.' How far do you agree? Explain your answer.

Conclusion: Henry VIII and Wolsey, 1509–29

How should we remember the young Henry VIII, 1509–29?

On page 12 we introduced Henry as a 'Renaissance Prince', a ruler excited by new ideas and possessing a wide range of talents. In some ways Henry did live up to this description in the first twenty years of his reign. Sir Thomas More later remembered how the King had summoned him to discuss new ideas about topics such as geometry and politics and that they used to go up on to the roof to look at the skies and talk about astronomy.

Yet, in most ways, there was nothing new about Henry VIII's approach to being king. His hero was Henry V, who won the Battle of Agincourt, and Henry's greatest wish was to win glory as a military leader, just like some earlier English kings. As you will see in Key Topic 2 he was also a great defender of the Roman Catholic Church against people who were criticising it. In 1521, the Pope even gave Henry the title *'Fidei Defensor'* (Defender of the Faith) because Henry had written a book defending the Catholic Church. You can still see this title on coins today.

In contrast, Henry did not send English ships to join other countries in exploring the Americas. He did not have any new ideas for government. He was very good at having fun

and he was ruthless in dealing with anyone who he thought had failed him. He had two of his father's advisers executed at the beginning of his reign to win popularity. He would, in all likelihood, have ordered the execution of Wolsey in 1530 despite all Wolsey's loyalty and efforts. It seems all that excitement in 1509 about the great new king had been a lot of fuss about very little.

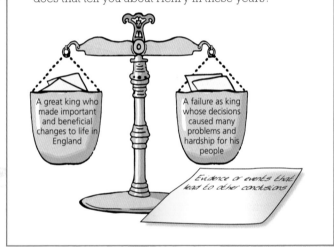

1. Think back over Chapters 1–4. Which of Henry's policies and the events that took place between 1509 and 1529 would you place on each side of the set of scales or on the sheet alongside?

2. If you cannot think of much to add to these scales, what does that tell you about Henry in these years?

A great king who made important and beneficial changes to life in England

A failure as king whose decisions caused many problems and hardship for his people

Evidence or events that lead to other conclusions

Was Wolsey a great and successful minister?

Now you have completed your work on Wolsey, this is the right time to sum up his achievements.

1. Draw your own copy of the continuum line below and decide where each of the events and policies on the cards should go on the line.
2. How would you describe Wolsey's career as Henry's Chief Minister?

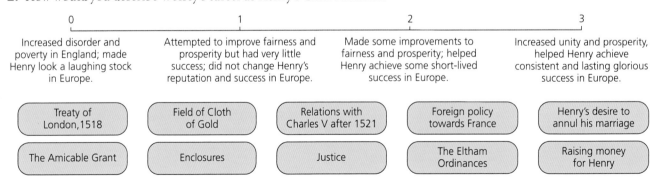

0	1	2	3
Increased disorder and poverty in England; made Henry look a laughing stock in Europe.	Attempted to improve fairness and prosperity but had very little success; did not change Henry's reputation and success in Europe.	Made some improvements to fairness and prosperity; helped Henry achieve some short-lived success in Europe.	Increased unity and prosperity, helped Henry achieve consistent and lasting glorious success in Europe.

Treaty of London, 1518

Field of Cloth of Gold

Relations with Charles V after 1521

Foreign policy towards France

Henry's desire to annul his marriage

The Amicable Grant

Enclosures

Justice

The Eltham Ordinances

Raising money for Henry

Visible learning: Revise and remember

'I do not need to worry about revision. There will be plenty of time for that before the exams.' You might agree with this thought, but before you turn over and ignore this revision page, take a look at the graphs below. They should convince you that leaving revision until just before your exam is not the way to success!

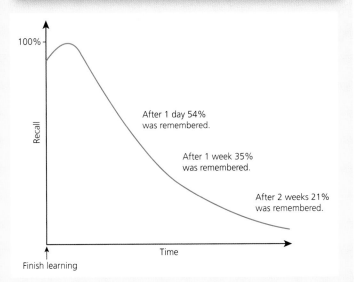

▲ Graph 1 The Ebbinghaus Curve of Forgetting. We forget the detail of what we study very quickly.

▲ Graph 2 How do you stop yourself forgetting?

1 Test yourself

You need to work at making your knowledge stick! The more you recap what you have learned and identify what you're not sure about, the more your chance of success. Answer these questions, and repeat those you don't know more frequently.

1. Why were some people delighted when Henry VIII became king?	2. In what year was the Field of Cloth of Gold?	3. What names were given to the new tax introduced by Wolsey?	4. Which event led to Charles V gaining control of Rome and the Pope?
5. When did Wolsey become Henry's Chancellor and Chief Minister?	6. Which king did Henry meet at the Field of Cloth of Gold?	7. List three activities that Henry VIII enjoyed for relaxation.	8. What were enclosures?
9. Give two reasons why the Church was important in sixteenth-century England.	10. What was the name of the daughter of Henry and Catherine of Aragon?	11. Describe three features of the Field of Cloth of Gold.	12. What did you find hardest to understand in this key topic? How are you going to help yourself understand it?

2 What's the question?

We have provided the answers below but it is your job to come up with suitable matching questions. Try to make each question as detailed as possible so you are using your knowledge to help you word it. This is a valuable way of revising because you have to think carefully about topics from a different angle.

1. King Francis I	2. Pope Clement VII
3. The Treaty of London	4. Jousting
5. Anne Boleyn	6. Prince Arthur
7. The Eltham Ordinances	8. Thomas Wolsey
9. The Amicable Grant	10. Annulment

Key Topics 2 and 3 investigate the 1530s, one of the most dramatic decades in English history. It was the decade when:

- England became a Protestant country after a thousand years of being part of the Catholic Church.
- Centuries-old monasteries, often providing care for the poor, were closed down.
- There was a great rebellion in the north and many people who opposed religious changes were executed.
- There was serious fear of invasion by France and the Holy Roman Empire.
- The way the country was governed began to change.
- King Henry, who had been married to one woman for twenty years, married four more wives in just seven years.

Take away these events and Henry VIII would probably not be studied in schools!

One of the men at the heart of these astonishing events was, as you would expect, Henry VIII. The other was a blacksmith's son called Thomas Cromwell who, during the 1530s, was the second most powerful man in England.

So many things happened in the 1530s that, to help you understand them more clearly, they are divided between Key Topics 2 and 3. Here is what they cover:

2. Henry VIII and Cromwell, 1529–40	3. The Reformation and its impact, 1529–40
How Cromwell rose to such great power.	The break from Rome and how it took place.
Why Henry made so many marriages.	Opposition to the Reformation and how it changed the Church.
How Cromwell changed the way England was governed.	The reasons for the Dissolution of the Monasteries and how it affected people.
Why Cromwell fell from power so suddenly and, like so many others, was executed.	Why the Pilgrimage of Grace broke out and why it ended.

Henry VIII in the 1530s

A great deal of Key Topics 2 and 3 will be about Thomas Cromwell, but the most powerful man in England was still Henry VIII. By the time Holbein painted this portrait Henry was 45 years old, no longer a young adventurous king. In particular, 1536 was a difficult year. Anne Boleyn was executed. The north of England exploded in rebellion against religious changes. Henry suffered a serious leg injury in a jousting accident when his horse fell on top of him. Walking became difficult, he put on weight and people noticed a change in his behaviour. He became angrier, less tolerant, more unpredictable.

HENRY VIII IN THE 1530S

1. Look carefully at the portrait of Henry VIII. Which of the following words best describe the person you see? (You can choose more than one or choose your own.)

   confident   arrogant   energetic   ruthless   determined   old

2. Compare this portrait of Henry with those on pages 3 and 13.
   a) What differences can you see in the way the portrait presents Henry?
   b) What reasons for the differences can you suggest?

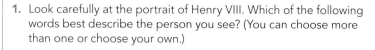

◀ Henry VIII, painted by Hans Holbein in 1537.

Introducing Thomas Cromwell

Thomas Cromwell was born in Putney in London around 1485. His father was at different times a blacksmith and a cloth-worker, but was never wealthy. Cromwell left home as a teenager and his travels provided his education. He fought in wars in Italy as a **mercenary soldier**. He worked for **merchants** in the Netherlands in the town of Antwerp, one of the great trading ports of Europe. By the time he returned to England in about 1512 he had military and commercial experience and was fluent in French and Italian.

Within a few years Cromwell was working for Cardinal Wolsey and by the early 1530s he had become the King's closest adviser. In 1534 he was appointed the King's Chief Minister and six years later the King made Cromwell a nobleman, the Earl of Essex. This was an astonishing achievement for a boy from a poor family but, within months, Cromwell lost all his power. In 1540 he was charged with treason and imprisoned in the Tower of London. From there he wrote to the King, ending 'Most gracious Prince, I cry for mercy, mercy, mercy!'

Henry showed no mercy. Cromwell was condemned to death without a trial. In July 1540, like so many others during the reign of Henry VIII, he was executed when an axeman struck his head from his body.

▲ Holbein's portrait of Cromwell from about 1532–34, when Cromwell was around 48 years old.

CROWMELL AND HENRY

1. Look carefully at this portrait of Cromwell. Which of the following words best describe the person you see? (You can choose more than one or choose your own.)

reliable	ambitious	dutiful	honest	emotional	ruthless

2. What does Cromwell's early life suggest about the type of man he was?
3. Think back to your work on Wolsey.
   a) What do you think Henry would expect of a new chief adviser after 1529?
   b) Who might have been jealous of Cromwell's rise to power?
   c) Why do you think Henry's advisers rarely felt secure in power?
4. Re-read these pages. Make a list of three good history questions you want to ask about Henry, Cromwell or the events of the 1530s.

> **WARNING!**
>
> DO NOT CONFUSE THOMAS CROMWELL WITH OLIVER CROMWELL!
>
> Thomas Cromwell was Henry VIII's Chief Minister in the 1530s. Oliver Cromwell was a parliamentary general during the English Civil War in the 1640s and Lord Protector of England in the 1650s.

The story of the 1530s

Pages 48–51 are the most important pages in the rest of this book. This is because they introduce the events in the 1530s which appear in Key Topics 2 and 3 and show *particularly how they are interconnected*. It may seem odd to split the events of one decade across two key topics but in the specification for this course the events of the 1530s are organised thematically, so this book follows that method of organisation – Key Topic 2 deals with Cromwell, Henry's marriages and changes in government, while Key Topic 3 explores the religious changes and their impact. However, you do need to understand the links between these themes. That is why the activities below are really important, because they enable you to see the outline of the key events of the 1530s and understand those connections.

Visible learning

Effective reading

The most effective way to read a section of text such as pages 48–51 is to read it twice – at least! The first time read it quickly to identify the main points. Don't worry too much about the detail. Then read it again, this time focusing on the detail that supports the main points. In each read through you have a clear purpose and this helps you read more effectively.

THE EVENTS OF THE 1530S

1. Draw a timeline running from 1509 to 1541. Place on it the beginning and the end of Henry's marriage to each of his first five wives.

   What does the pattern on this timeline tell you?

2. Draw your own copy of the timeline below, giving yourself plenty of space. Use the information on pages 48–51 to record the major events of 1529–40 on your timeline.

Religious events

1528	1532	1534	1536	1538	1540

Political events and royal marriages

3. Work with a partner to read pages 48–51 and explain the connections OR the similarities between the pairs in the bingo card below.
   a) Your first task is to complete a line of pairs.
   b) Second, compete to see who first gets a full house of correct answers.

1	The King's Great Matter AND Henry becoming Supreme Head of the Church of England.	**2**	The King's Great Matter AND the execution of Thomas More.	**3**	The Church of England AND the fear of invasion.
4	The Dissolution of the Monasteries AND one other event.	**5**	The execution of John Fisher AND the Pilgrimage of Grace.	**6**	The Church of England AND changes in the role of Parliament.
7	Fear of invasion AND Henry's marriage to Anne of Cleves.	**8**	Fear of invasion AND Cromwell's execution.	**9**	Anne Boleyn AND Catherine Howard.

4. Identify two similarities and two differences between the work and careers of Wolsey and Cromwell.

Ending a marriage, starting a Church

By 1529 the King's Great Matter – Henry's desire to end his marriage to Catherine of Aragon – was dominating political events but the Pope was refusing to annul the marriage. The Pope's refusal led directly to Henry and Cromwell creating the new Church of England. In the early 1530s, under Cromwell's guidance, Henry broke England's connection to the Roman Catholic Church. Between 1532 and 1534 a series of Acts of Parliament gave the King control over Church taxes, legal cases and appointments of bishops and archbishops. In 1533 Henry appointed Thomas Cranmer as Archbishop of Canterbury. Cranmer now had the power to say that Henry's marriage to Catherine was invalid and that he was free to marry Anne Boleyn.

Finally, in 1534, the Act of Supremacy declared the King 'Supreme Head of the Church of England'. Everyone had to take an oath recognising Henry as Head of the Church. Anyone who did not take the oath risked being charged with treason.

Marriage to Anne Boleyn

Henry married Anne Boleyn in January 1533. The marriage was hastily arranged because Anne was pregnant and the child would only be legitimate if Henry and Anne were married. However, the longed-for child turned out to be a girl (Elizabeth). When a second pregnancy miscarried in 1536, Henry lost hope that Anne would give him a male heir and interpreted her failure to produce boys as evidence that God was displeased with this marriage. Henry was now falling for Jane Seymour, and again Cromwell solved the King's problem. Anne Boleyn was accused of infidelity, found guilty of treason – thanks to evidence acquired by Cromwell – and executed in May 1536.

Opposition, monasteries and rebellion

Many people opposed the changes Cromwell made to the Church but few had the courage to oppose Cromwell and Henry. Three individuals who dared make a stand against religious change were Elizabeth Barton (the 'Nun of Kent'), Sir Thomas More and John Fisher, the Bishop of Rochester. All were executed for their opposition.

The Dissolution of the Monasteries between 1536 and 1540 created much more widespread opposition. In 1530 there were over 800 monasteries in England and Wales, and their wealth attracted Henry and Cromwell's attention. They needed money for defence because of the fear of invasion by France and the Empire to restore Catholicism to England. Cromwell orchestrated a government campaign of intimidation against the monasteries, accusing monks and nuns of not keeping their monastic vows of chastity, poverty and obedience. Cromwell's evidence persuaded Parliament to close the monasteries and confiscate their wealth.

The Dissolution was a major cause of the rebellion known as the Pilgrimage of Grace in 1536 – 30,000 people joined the rising across the north so it was a very real threat to Henry. However, a combination of royal trickery and force ended the rising and the leaders were executed.

A son for Henry, reform for Cromwell

Henry married Jane Seymour within two weeks of Anne being beheaded. In 1537 Jane gave birth to a son who was called Edward. Henry was distraught when Jane died from complications during the birth.

During the mid-1530s Cromwell changed some important aspects of government. Parliament met much more frequently to pass the Acts making the religious changes legal and to give the impression that the nation was united behind the King. This helped give Parliament a more important part in government. Some historians also believe that Cromwell strengthened royal power and created a more 'modern' structure for government based around properly organised departments rather than everything being run from the Royal Household.

The end of Cromwell

Henry married again in 1540. His fourth wife was Anne of Cleves, the daughter of the Duke of Cleves, a small state in Germany. She was recommended by Cromwell to win Cleves as an ally and so reduce fears of invasion by Catholic countries. Unfortunately, Henry took an immediate dislike to Anne and the fear of invasion disappeared so Henry blamed Cromwell for a marriage he did not want. Henry's anger gave Cromwell's enemies at Court the opportunity to destroy him.

The Duke of Norfolk, the uncle of Anne Boleyn, now suggested that Henry marry another of his nieces, 17-year-old Catherine Howard. Henry's marriage to Anne of Cleves was annulled in July 1540 and he married Catherine in August. This marriage failed too. In November 1541 Henry received evidence that Catherine had been unfaithful and she was executed for treason in 1542.

By then Cromwell was dead, executed for treason in July 1540. His enemies had won. Henry remained king for another seven years but never trusted anyone to replace Cromwell as his most trusted adviser.

HENRY AND CROMWELL – SUCCESS OR FAILURE?

At the end of Key Topics 2 and 3 (page 111) we will again return to our overall question – **Was Henry VIII a successful king?** However, at the same time we need to assess Cromwell's achievements.

1. Use the information on these pages to pencil in your first thoughts about topics which could go in column 3 in the table below.

2. As you work through Key Topics 2 and 3 you can review these ideas and add more detail to your table.

Henry and Cromwell's successes	Henry and Cromwell's failures	Topics or events that could be seen as either success or failure	Who was most responsible for each success or failure – Henry or Cromwell?

TELLING YOUR OWN STORY OF THE 1530s

This activity will help you consolidate the story of the 1530s in your memory.

1 The illustrations below show five scenes from the 1530s. What is shown in each illustration?

2 Choose THREE other important events from the period 1530–1540 that have been omitted from these illustrations.

3 Write your own account of the events of 1530–1540 in no more than 200 words.

Henry VIII and Cromwell, 1529–40

5 Cromwell's rise to power and the King's marriages

5.1 Why did Henry make Cromwell his Chief Minister?

Cromwell returned from abroad in around 1512 when he was about 27. He had military and commercial experience and was fluent in French and Italian. He trained as a lawyer and around 1524 he was employed by Thomas Wolsey, the King's Chief Minister. Joining Wolsey's staff was a major turning point in Cromwell's career. He was soon working as Wolsey's legal adviser, so Wolsey clearly trusted Cromwell's legal and administrative knowledge and skills. Perhaps Wolsey, a butcher's son, also admired a man who, like himself, had made good from obscure origins.

During the 1520s Cromwell showed the qualities that played a major part in his rise. He was clever, knowledgeable and a very good administrator. In addition he stood by his beliefs even if he disagreed with the King. In 1523 he became a Member of Parliament (MP) when Henry was planning to invade France. Cromwell did not believe England had the money or the army to launch a successful invasion. A document still exists showing that Cromwell wrote a speech attacking the idea of an invasion. We do not know if he made the speech in Parliament, but it shows he was willing to argue against the King.

Wolsey's downfall in 1529–30 threatened Cromwell's career, but his loyalty to Wolsey was noted by the King. Henry must have been surrounded by yes men who told him what they thought he wanted to hear. In contrast, Cromwell's support for Wolsey when everyone else was attacking him made Cromwell stand out as a man of strong character and great loyalty.

Working for Wolsey created opportunities for Cromwell, but he was still a long way from being the King's Chief Minister. Between 1529 and 1532 Henry seems to have made his own decisions, but hesitated to make a decisive break from Rome. During these years Cromwell gradually came to the attention of the King and by 1534 he was Henry's Chief Minister. The tasks below help you explain why Henry chose Cromwell for this role.

CROMWELL'S RISE TO POWER

1. Draw your own spider diagram like the one shown here to record the reasons why Henry made Cromwell his Chief Minister.
   a) Add to your diagram in pencil any qualities you have already read about that helped Cromwell become Chief Minister.
   b) Read through pages 53–55 quickly, then add more reasons to your diagram for Henry choosing Cromwell.
   c) Re-read these pages more carefully. Revise your diagram and collect evidence of each reason in a table such as the one below.

Reasons for Henry's choice of Cromwell as Chief Minister	Evidence of Cromwell's qualities or actions which led to the appointment
1.	

Why did Henry make Cromwell his Chief Minister?

The King's annulment – solving Henry's problems

The key to Cromwell's rise to power was his ability to solve Henry's problem – how to annul his marriage to Catherine of Aragon. In 1532, six years after falling in love with Anne Boleyn, Henry was still married to Catherine of Aragon and still didn't have a legitimate son. The Pope was still refusing to annul the marriage and no amount of pressure had changed his mind. This search for the annulment was 'the King's Great Matter' – and Cromwell succeeded where Wolsey had failed. These were the main steps along Cromwell's path to solving Henry's marriage problem:

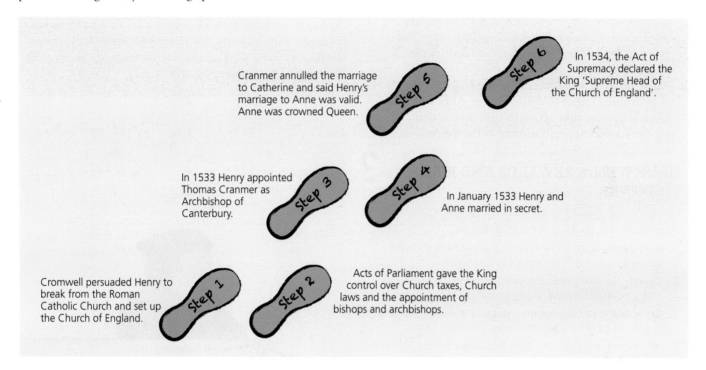

Step 5
Cranmer annulled the marriage to Catherine and said Henry's marriage to Anne was valid. Anne was crowned Queen.

Step 6
In 1534, the Act of Supremacy declared the King 'Supreme Head of the Church of England'.

Step 3
In 1533 Henry appointed Thomas Cranmer as Archbishop of Canterbury.

Step 4
In January 1533 Henry and Anne married in secret.

Step 1
Cromwell persuaded Henry to break from the Roman Catholic Church and set up the Church of England.

Step 2
Acts of Parliament gave the King control over Church taxes, Church laws and the appointment of bishops and archbishops.

Cromwell's qualities

What qualities enabled Cromwell to impress Henry and plan the annulment of his marriage?

Legal training and experience. Cromwell was a lawyer with lots of experience working for Cardinal Wolsey. This meant that he understood how to get things done quickly and effectively. For example, in May 1532 he forced the Church to accept the King and not the Pope as their lawmaker. This was a sure way to identify his opponents.

Experience as an MP in Parliament. Cromwell knew how to manage Parliament to get it to do what the King wanted. Bribes, threats, legal arguments and patronage (buying support with rewards of land or money) were used to persuade and also to force Parliament to make the necessary reforms.

Religious views. Cromwell had no very strong religious views, but his sympathies were with the Protestants. A man who was loyal to the Catholic Church could not have steered Parliament to transfer power over the English Church from the Pope to the King. The clergy were forced to accept Henry as the Head of the English Church, to stop paying Church taxes to Rome and to submit to the King's authority over all Church laws.

Cromwell's loyalty to Henry. Cromwell's personality made him a faithful and loyal servant, prepared to do whatever was needed to help King Henry. For example, he was ruthless in prosecuting and executing those people who refused to accept Henry as the Supreme Head of the Church.

Cromwell's intelligence and inventiveness. Cromwell was a very intelligent man who understood power politics. His years in Europe had taught him about warfare, religion and finances – the sorts of things that princes cared about. He was very inventive in finding solutions to problems: for example, the Dissolution of the Monasteries (see page 96) was probably an idea that no one else would have thought of, because it was so drastic.

Was it only Cromwell?

Cromwell was Henry's 'Mr Fix-it', the man he relied on to get things done. Cromwell's qualities helped him guide the King through the legal, religious and personal minefield of the 1530s.

However, it would be a mistake to think that Cromwell alone was responsible for solving the King's problem.

- **Thomas Cranmer:** In 1532 Henry appointed a new Archbishop of Canterbury, Thomas Cranmer. He wanted the Church reformed along Protestant lines (see Key Topic 3) and urged Henry to control the English Church.
- **Anne Boleyn:** As a Protestant, Anne had no qualms about urging Henry to defy the Pope. Anne's pregnancy forced Henry to take action to ensure their child was legitimate and so could succeed to the throne.

Cromwell's influence over Henry

Henry was his own master and in the 1530s Cromwell did not enjoy as much influence over the King as Wolsey once had. Nevertheless, Henry grew to trust Cromwell's judgement. Cromwell also understood how to suggest ideas to the King in such a way that Henry thought they were *his* ideas. This was important in dealing with a man with an ego as big as Henry VIII's. Henry and Cromwell worked together very closely, and Cromwell took much of the burden of kingship from Henry's shoulders. There was always the risk, though, that Cromwell might appear over-familiar with the King, or that Henry might grow to resent Cromwell's command of his affairs.

CROMWELL'S REWARDS AND RISE TO POWER ?

Henry VIII was grateful to Cromwell for helping him solve these problems. Looking at the steps below:

1. Identify two appointments which particularly showed Henry's increasing confidence in Cromwell.

2. Identify two appointments which enabled Cromwell to make money to match his rise in status.

3. Complete your diagram from page 52 summing up why Cromwell became Chief Minister.

4. Which two reasons were most important in Cromwell's rise to Chief Minister? Explain your choices.

Principal Secretary, 1534
This confirmed Cromwell as Henry's Chief Minister.

Chancellor of the Exchequer, 1533
Cromwell was now responsible for collecting royal revenue. This was a position of the highest responsibility, previously held by Sir Thomas More (who resigned in 1532) and Cardinal Wolsey.

Clerk of the Hanaper, 1532
The Clerk was paid fees for the sealing of charters, writs and patents using the Great Seal, which was used to stamp royal documents.

Master of the King's Jewel House, 1532
The Crown Jewels are the symbols of the King's power and authority. Trusting them to Cromwell showed how much faith Henry had in him. It also gave him an annual payment.

Lordship of Romney in Newport, Wales, 1532
One example of a reward from the King that gave Cromwell social and political status. It was also another source of income.

Membership of the Royal Council, 1530
The Royal Council was the King's small council of trusted advisers. Membership gave Cromwell the opportunity to influence the King's most important decisions.

Cromwell's role as the King's Chief Minister

Henry trusted Cromwell to make sure that royal policies were respected and observed. Cromwell was Henry's 'enforcer', making sure everyone submitted to Henry's authority. There is one paragraph written by Cromwell in the Act of Appeals of 1533 that sums up Cromwell's job. He had to ensure that this statement was true:

> England is an independent national state, and has been recognised as such throughout history. It is governed by one – and only one – person, the King of England, free from any outside authority. All the people who live within its borders, regardless of their wealth or status, if they are clergy or laymen, are equally his subjects. They all owe the king their undivided loyalty and obedience to his laws and commands.

CROMWELL'S ROLE AS CHIEF MINISTER

1. Why did Henry VIII need a Chief Minister?
2. Read the paragraph from the Act of Appeals (left).
   a) What was so important about each of these phrases?
      i) 'free from any outside authority'
      ii) 'They all owe the King their undivided loyalty'
   b) Why was it so important for Cromwell to enforce the details of this paragraph in the Act of Appeals?
3. Explain Cromwell's objectives as Chief Minister.

Establish the King's power over the Church

Cromwell had to make sure that the English Church accepted the King's authority. He oversaw changes in doctrine and church services that were in more of a Protestant style and he organised the Dissolution of the Monasteries.

Enforce loyalty and obedience to Henry

Cromwell had to deal with opposition to Henry's policies, including the Pilgrimage of Grace (see page 101) and individual opponents of the King's authority such as Sir Thomas More, the Maid of Kent and Bishop Fisher. All three of these individuals were executed, as was Robert Aske, the leader of the Pilgrimage of Grace.

Cromwell's role as Chief Minister

Make the King's power greater and government more efficient

Cromwell strengthened royal authority throughout the country. He united England and Wales by incorporating Wales into the English legal and administrative system. This ended the separate identity of Wales, which now sent 24 Members of Parliament to Westminster. He strengthened the role of Parliament and ensured the King got his way in Parliament. He reformed the administration of the government, partly to ensure that the King received more income.

Defending England from foreign interference and rule

Like Wolsey before him, Cromwell took control of English foreign policy, which meant England's relations with the Holy Roman Empire, with France, and with the Pope. He needed to ensure that no other state challenged or reduced Henry's power.

5.2 Why was Anne Boleyn executed in 1536?

Just three years after Henry and Anne Boleyn were married, Anne was executed at the Tower of London. What could possibly have gone so wrong that the King had his wife beheaded? Henry had broken with a thousand years of religious tradition and risked war with the Catholic powers to annul his marriage to Catherine and marry Anne. He had been besotted with Anne, so why did she die?

Pages 56–59 investigate why Anne was executed. It starts with the story of Anne's fall. The time-chart opposite sets out the story in a different way.

What happened to Anne Boleyn?

Queen Anne gave birth to Henry's child on 7 September 1533, a girl who was called Elizabeth. If Anne had given birth to a healthy boy it is likely that her marriage to Henry would have continued until one of them died naturally. The Succession to the Crown Act of 1534 said that the Crown would pass to Elizabeth on Henry's death, assuming he had no male heir. There was every possibility that Anne would have another pregnancy and give birth to a healthy boy.

In 1535, however, the relationship between Henry and Anne began to break down. Henry had noticed Jane Seymour, one of Anne's ladies-in-waiting. Jane was quiet and demure, exactly as women were expected to be. In contrast, Anne was vivacious and sensuous but Henry was tiring of her bossiness and demands.

In January 1536 Anne suffered a miscarriage, shattering Henry's hopes for a son. Henry did not regard his failure to produce a son as an accident or as anything to do with him. Instead he began to ask whether God was now punishing him for his marriage to Anne.

The end was swift. On 1 May Henry and Anne attended a May Day joust at Greenwich. Part-way through the tournament, Henry suddenly rose and left, leaving the Queen behind. His courtiers, one of whom was Henry Norris, raced to accompany him. On the way into London Norris was arrested and taken to the Tower, where he was charged with treason.

Anne must have been filled with dread. On the previous day one of her court musicians, Mark Smeaton, had been arrested and charged with treason. Anne could not have known it yet, but Mark Smeaton was pouring out to Cromwell a tale of adultery and incest concerning Henry's queen. Five men were accused of adultery with Anne, including her own brother, Lord Rochford. The charge made sense. Anne was naturally flirtatious and attractive, and encouraged the men around her to pay her compliments. Cromwell interrogated the accused men separately, and may have used torture on Mark Smeaton to obtain the first confession. No one really knows if there was any truth in these accusations, but true or false,

▲ Anne Boleyn, who was described as having a long neck, wide mouth and 'eyes which were black and beautiful'.

Anne Boleyn was doomed. Her trial was held on 15 May, and she was found guilty.

On 19 May 1536 Anne Boleyn was executed. A French swordsman was brought over to carry out the execution. Henry wanted Anne's death to be quick and to draw little public attention. Anne was led to the scaffold at 8 o'clock in the morning. She made a short speech before kneeling down, where she began to pray. The swordsman distracted her by calling for his sword, causing Anne to turn her head slightly, which gave the executioner a clean target. With one blow she was beheaded.

THE FALL OF ANNE BOLEYN

1. Use the text on this page and the time-chart on page 57 to identify evidence or events that show:
   a) Henry's continued commitment to Queen Anne
   b) Henry's growing interest in Jane Seymour.
2. Which event appears to be the main turning point in Henry's relationship with Anne?
3. What word or words would you use to describe the speed of Anne's fall from power?
4. What role did Thomas Cromwell play in her fall?

1533	
January	Henry and Anne married in secret
June	Anne crowned Queen
September	Anne gave birth to a daughter, Elizabeth
1534	
March	Succession of the Crown Act made Princess Elizabeth Henry's heir
1536	
January	Anne miscarried a male child
April	Cromwell gave up his apartment at Greenwich Palace for Jane Seymour's use
April 24	Henry established a commission to investigate Anne's behaviour
30	Mark Smeaton arrested and confessed to adultery with Anne

May 1–4	Arrests of Henry Norris, Queen Anne, Lord Rochford, Sir Francis Weston and William Brereton
12–15	Trials of Queen Anne, Norris, Weston, Brereton and Rochford
17	Rochford, Norris, Weston, Brereton and Smeaton executed
	Henry's marriage to Anne declared null and void on the grounds that Anne's sister, Mary, had been Henry's mistress
19	Anne Boleyn executed
30	Henry married Jane Seymour

Your enquiry: Why was Anne Boleyn executed?

On the surface, the reason Anne was executed is because she had committed adultery, which meant that, as Queen, she had committed treason by betraying Henry. However, you need to be careful with this kind of simple explanation. Like an iceberg, there is more to the answer than meets the eye! Hidden below the surface of Anne's trial, there were other reasons why she was executed. Some of these reasons might be more important than the reason given in court.

1. Make a large copy of the iceberg diagram shown here. What other reasons do you think played a part in Anne's execution from your reading of this page? Pencil those reasons on to your diagram in the lower part of the iceberg.
2. Read page 58.
   a) Identify and add reasons for Anne's execution to your iceberg diagram. Give each reason a short heading.
   b) Complete a table like the one below, identifying how each reason helped lead to Anne's execution. One example has been done for you.

Reason 1
Anne was found guilty of adultery.

Other reasons

Reasons for Anne's execution	How did this reason help explain Anne's execution?
1. Anne was found guilty of adultery	If the Queen committed adultery this was treason because she had been disloyal to the King. Treason was punished with execution.

Why was Anne Boleyn executed?

These reasons (A–F) for Anne's execution are not in chronological order or in order of importance.

A. Anne's downfall was dangerous for Cromwell. He had worked with Anne to secure her marriage to Henry. Now that Henry wanted to get rid of her, Cromwell feared the King would blame him for his marriage to Anne. There were also plenty of courtiers (including the Duke of Norfolk) who resented Cromwell's power and would be happy to see him destroyed. Therefore Cromwell had to show he was still the man who could solve Henry's problems by finding a way to end Henry's marriage to Anne swiftly.

B. Henry wanted a son to succeed him to ensure the continuation of the Tudor dynasty, but Anne had failed to provide him with a son. Henry had begun to wonder whether this was a punishment from God, and if the only way he could ever have a son would be to end this marriage and make a fresh start with a new, legal wife.

C. Henry was attracted to Jane Seymour, one of Anne's ladies-in-waiting. Jane was gentle and quiet – the model of the Tudor ideal of what women should be like. She seemed much more the ideal wife for a king and more likely to have a son.

D. In earlier years Anne and Cromwell had worked together but that collaboration had ended. For example, in April 1536 one of Anne's courtiers denounced Cromwell as the Queen's enemy in front of the entire Court. Anne also accused Cromwell of putting the money gained from the Dissolution of the Monasteries into the Royal Treasury instead of giving it to the poor. This attempt by Anne to denounce Cromwell for corruption backfired as it meant that Cromwell needed to remove Anne to defend his own position.

E. Anne's downfall was partly a result of international events. Since the split with Rome there had been an increased sense of foreign danger. It was feared that the Emperor Charles V would invade England because of the break from Rome and Henry's treatment of the Emperor's aunt, Queen Catherine. Cromwell was anxious to improve relations with the Empire but this was near-impossible while Anne was Henry's queen. Anne was getting in the way of Cromwell's diplomacy and seemed to be increasing the likelihood of invasion.

F. Anne was accused of not only adultery but also of 'Imagining the king's death', which sounds as if she planned to kill Henry. However 'Imagining the king's death' could be as simple as saying, 'If the king were to die without a clear line of succession, then…' or 'when Princess Elizabeth is queen…' Simply imagining a world in which the King had died was treason – and it gave Cromwell the opportunity to solve Henry's marriage problem for him.

Communicating your answer

The biggest mistake that students make is to write their answer without having the answer clear in their heads. These activities help you avoid doing that and they will work better if you do them with a partner.

1. Return to your iceberg diagram and your table of reasons from page 57. Make sure your iceberg diagram includes all the reasons for Anne Boleyn's execution.

2. Now you have identified the reasons, what links can you see between them?

   a) Draw the chart below, then write the reasons for Anne's execution into the boxes.

   b) Draw at least two lines to show connections between pairs of reasons.

   c) Explain the links by annotating the lines you have drawn.

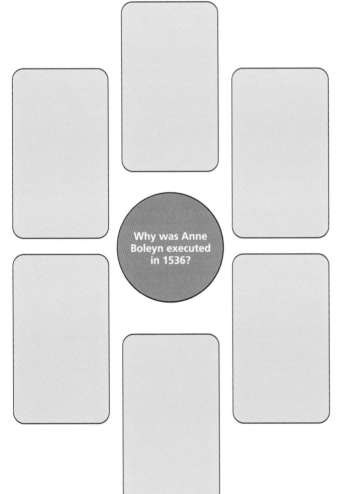

Why was Anne Boleyn executed in 1536?

3. Historians often divide the causes of an event into three categories:

Long-term causes	Short-term causes	Triggers

   a) Now you have a good understanding of the reasons for Anne's execution, decide if using these categories helps you explain her execution more effectively.

   b) If the answers to part (a) is 'yes', place the reasons for Anne's execution in each of these categories.

4. Now write a paragraph summarising your answer to the question:

Explain why Anne Boleyn was executed in 1536.

5. Now it's time to write a full answer to the question. This chapter has given you a good deal of help but you will find more guidance in the Writing Better History guide on pages 112–22. However, the person who will give you the best advice is your teacher because he or she knows exactly what help you need to improve your work in History. One of the ways of doing this is to choose appropriate words when you write. The Word Wall below will help you with this.

Updating your Word Wall

These words will help you answer questions on topics in this chapter in your exam. Therefore you need to understand all of them – can you explain why each of them could be useful?

adultery   legitimate   miscarried

treason   patronage   demure

Chancellor   Dissolution   Privy Council

Principal Secretary   Supreme Head

Practice questions

1. Describe two features of:
   a) his personality that helped Cromwell become Chief Minister
   b) Cromwell's work as Chief Minister
   c) Cromwell's role in the fall of Anne Boleyn.
2. Explain why Cromwell rose to power to be King Henry's Chief Minister.
3. 'The main reason for Anne Boleyn's execution was that she did not give birth to a son.' How far do you agree? Explain your answer.

5.3 Jane Seymour – marriage, birth and death

Henry's marriage to Jane Seymour was encouraged by Cromwell, so much so that you could almost call Cromwell the match-maker. He organised a royal visit to Wiltshire in the summer of 1535, during which Henry stayed at Wulfhall, the Seymour family home. Nobody really knows, but this might have been the occasion when Henry really noticed Jane. At Easter 1536 Cromwell gave up his apartment at Greenwich Palace for Jane to use. Those rooms were connected to Henry's by secret passages. Just a few weeks later, on 30 May 1536, Jane married the King. By now Catherine of Aragon had died and Anne Boleyn had been executed. There was no doubt that this marriage was legal.

Jane Seymour was intelligent, sympathetic and popular. She worked hard to bring about a reconciliation between Henry and his first daughter, Mary, though she failed to get Mary restored to the line of succession. Henry was taken with Jane's gentleness, but told her not to interfere with matters of state when she urged him to be merciful to the leaders of the Pilgrimage of Grace (see page 101).

In August 1537, Cromwell's son Gregory married Queen Jane's sister, Elizabeth. Cromwell was now related to the King, even if distantly by marriage. Cromwell may have felt this gave him security, as an attack on Cromwell by jealous noblemen would now be an attack on the King's family.

Cromwell had an even greater reason to think that his position as Henry's Chief Minister was now secure when, on 12 October 1537, Jane Seymour gave birth to a healthy boy.

Henry named him Edward in honour of Henry's own grandfather, King Edward IV. Within hours of his birth a proclamation was issued in the Queen's name announcing the birth of 'a Prince conceived in Lawful Matrimony'. At long last the Tudor dynasty was secure.

Then, disaster struck. Jane's labour had been difficult, lasting three days and two nights. Three days after giving birth, Jane fell ill and on 24 October she died. Her death posed a whole new set of problems for Cromwell. It broke his family connection with Henry, who would now expect Cromwell to negotiate another marriage – Henry's fourth – on his behalf. Cromwell's position, which had recently seemed so secure, had suddenly become more vulnerable.

Thomas Cromwell
|
Henry VIII = Jane Seymour   Elizabeth Seymour = Gregory Cromwell

SISTERS

▲ Cromwell's new marriage link to the royal family.

Will the King expect a new wife?

I have lost my family link to the King

Thomas Cromwell

JANE SEYMOUR

1. Read pages 60–61. Identify four crucial events in the story of Jane Seymour and add them to a diagram like the one below.

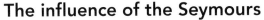

2. How did Henry's marriage to Jane first increase then decrease Cromwell's security as Chief Minister?
3. How did Jane's brothers benefit from her marriage to the King?

The influence of the Seymours

Jane had two brothers, who benefited from suddenly becoming part of the royal family.

Edward Seymour (top right) was already well known to King Henry before the marriage to Jane. Edward had fought in Henry's wars in France in the 1520s and had become one of the King's Esquires of the Body, one of his closest attendants who spent a lot of time with the King at Court. Soon after Henry married Jane, Edward was well rewarded. He was made Viscount Beauchamp and a member of the Royal Council. King Henry's trust in Edward was shown when Edward was asked to carry Princess Elizabeth at Prince Edward's baptism and was made Earl of Hertford, joining the great nobility.

Although his influence reduced after Jane's death, he still played a major part in military affairs during Henry's reign. Edward later became Lord Protector in the reign of King Edward VI, though rivalries with other nobles led to his execution.

Thomas Seymour (bottom right) was also one of Henry's courtiers in the early 1530s and gained considerably from the royal marriage. He was given lands and offices by the King, was knighted and took part in jousting tournaments. After King Henry died in 1547 Thomas married his widow, Catherine Parr, but his ambitions led to him, too, being executed in 1549.

Both men had gained a great deal from their sister's marriage. Even the great Duke of Norfolk wanted his daughter to marry Thomas Seymour, a sign that the Seymours were seen as a very influential family. However, the marriage never took place. The influence faded after Jane's death but they had made an important step up in status.

CONCLUDING THIS CHAPTER – SUCCESSES AND FAILURES

You can now update your table of successes and failures that was introduced on page 51 (shown again below). Where would you put each of these topics and how would you complete the table?

| Ending Henry's marriage to Queen Catherine | Splitting from the Church of Rome | Arranging the King's marriage to Anne Boleyn | Ending the King's marriage to Anne Boleyn | Arranging the King's marriage to Jane Seymour |

Henry and Cromwell's successes	Henry and Cromwell's failures	Topics or events that could be seen as either success or failure	Who was most responsible for each success or failure – Henry or Cromwell?

6 Thomas Cromwell, 1534–40

After Anne Boleyn's death, Thomas Cromwell served as Henry's Chief Minister for another four years, supervising rapid changes in government and in religion including the Dissolution of the Monasteries. Cromwell steered England through this period of change and he was richly rewarded by Henry. However, in 1540 everything went wrong for Cromwell. In less than two months, Cromwell was first arrested and accused of treason, then executed. His rise and his fall were as dramatic as Wolsey's had been.

This chapter is divided into two enquiries:

Enquiry 1: Did Cromwell make the King's government more effective?

Enquiry 2: Why was Thomas Cromwell executed in 1540?

6.1 Cromwell's reforms of the King's government

Cromwell's job was to make Henry's government more effective. This meant making sure that:

- crimes were punished effectively throughout the kingdom
- all regions of the kingdom were under control
- the King had money for war and other expenses
- Parliament passed the laws that were needed and did not oppose the King.

CROMWELL'S DECISIONS

This activity introduces four ways in which Cromwell tried to make Henry's government more efficient. Which options would you take in Cromwell's shoes – and why? Thinking about the reasons is the purpose of this activity.

Decision 1: Crime and justice

There were areas in the country where the King's officials could not arrest criminals. These places sometimes included churches, where criminals could take **sanctuary** and be free from arrest. Should Cromwell:

a) allow this to continue to avoid offending the Church even more?

b) make reforms to ensure criminals could be arrested everywhere?

c) ignore this issue because it was more important to focus on religious reform and dealing with the opponents of religious reform?

Decision 3: Royal finance

Henry needed money, especially to pay for defence as there was great anxiety about an invasion by Catholic countries. Which of these actions should Cromwell take?

a) Sell off the lands taken from the monasteries to fill the King's war chest quickly.

b) Keep the monastery lands because rents paid by farmers would continue to give the King income.

c) Leave monasteries as they are to reduce opposition and the possibility of invasion.

Decision 2: Royal power

The King did not have complete control throughout his kingdom. In places distant from London (Wales, Ireland and the North of England) there was lawlessness or the risk of rebellion. Should Cromwell:

a) make changes to give the king complete control in these areas?

b) do nothing because of the cost of taking control?

c) make some changes which reduced the danger of rebellion?

Decision 4: Parliament

Parliament was meeting more often but some MPs did not like the religious changes. Should Cromwell:

a) record how MPs voted so they felt under pressure to vote the way Henry wanted?

b) interfere in elections to make sure the elected MPs would support the religious changes?

c) warn lords not to attend Parliament if they were going to oppose the King?

6.2 Your enquiry: Did Cromwell make the King's government more effective?

On pages 64–67 you are going to assess the effectiveness of Cromwell's reforms of English government. The four areas to investigate are:

1. Crime and justice
2. Royal power
3. Royal finance
4. Parliament

After you have studied each area, place it on the continuum line below. This records your judgements on two things:

a) the effectiveness of the reform of each individual area
b) which area or areas were reformed most effectively.

0	1	2	3
Ineffective. Cromwell's reforms failed to achieve any improvement in this area.	Partly effective. Cromwell's reforms made some improvement but left the basic problem unchanged.	Mostly effective. Cromwell's reforms made a big difference to this area of government but did not solve the whole problem.	Very effective. Cromwell's reform of this topic solved the problem the King faced.

Collecting evidence

Before you can make your judgements about the effectiveness of these reforms you have to collect evidence about each reform. You need the evidence to justify your final decisions. Use your own copy of the table below to collect and summarise your evidence, and also make detailed notes in addition to this summary.

1. Draw a large copy of the table below. As you read the text fill in your answers to columns 2–4.
2. Use the level descriptors on the continuum line above to decide how effective each reform was, then complete column 5 by writing a brief explanation of your choice of level.

1. Problems	2. Cromwell's solutions	3. Information that shows effectiveness of reforms	4. Information that shows reforms did not solve problem	5. How effective? (0–3)
Crime and justice Ancient laws meant there were places where criminals could escape justice.				
Royal power The King did not have enough control over Ireland, Wales and the north of England.				
Royal finance More money was needed for defence in case of invasion.				
Parliament There was danger of Parliament opposing Henry's religious changes.				

THINK BACK AND CONNECT – WOLSEY AND CROMWELL

Wolsey had tried to improve government but none of his plans had been great successes. Now Cromwell wanted to reform government and he had more distractions than Wolsey. Could he achieve what Wolsey had failed to achieve?

a) What distractions had prevented Wolsey's government reforms being more successful?

b) What distractions did Cromwell have to deal with?

c) What qualities would Cromwell need to make these reforms a success?

▲ The Sanctuary Knocker at Durham Cathedral. If fugitives from justice grabbed the knocker, they could not be arrested. They could stay in the cathedral for forty days but then had to choose between standing trial or leaving England and going into exile. If they chose exile they walked to the coast carrying a white cross to show that they were sanctuary-men and could not be arrested.

Crime and justice

Given Henry VIII's fearsome reputation, it is easy to assume that the King's laws applied to every person in every part of the kingdom, and that royal officials could make arrests everywhere. This was not the case.

Churches, for example, were sanctuaries where people could not be arrested. As long as escaping criminals remained within the church walls, they were safe from arrest. The existence of these sanctuaries was often centuries-old, a reminder of the power of the Church.

There were also other areas in the kingdom, known as liberties, where the King's officers could not make arrests. Often these were places where the local lord had been given the right to hold trials and punish criminals, often with fines, so these lords wanted to keep these rights.

These old customs made a mockery of the King's authority, damaging his reputation as the defender of his people from crime and disorder. Other royal ministers might have tried to abolish these medieval places of sanctuary one by one, but that was not Cromwell's way.

Cromwell's solutions

1. In 1536 he made sure that Parliament abolished the liberties, all in one go.

2. Now that Henry was the Supreme Head of the Church in England, it was much easier to abolish the right of Church sanctuary. In 1540 an Act of Parliament abolished the right of sanctuary for serious crimes like rape and murder. However, it did not abolish sanctuary immediately for all less serious crimes.

CRIME AND JUSTICE ❓

1. Complete your table from page 63, collecting evidence for Cromwell's effectiveness and reaching your judgement.

2. Look back to Decision 1 on page 62. Did Cromwell choose one of the options – or something different?

Royal power

It had always been difficult for kings to control the distant parts of the kingdom. One reason was that transport and communications were slow so a rebellion could be well underway before the King heard about it. Second, the King did not have his own army but relied on his nobles to provide men to fight and deal with rebellions. Raising such an army was also slow and could be very expensive. Therefore rebellions and law-breaking in Ireland, Wales and the north of England could develop into a great threat to the King's power.

a) Ireland

England only controlled a small area around Dublin known as the Pale. The Anglo-Irish lords were the real power in Ireland.

Henry and Cromwell were far from happy with the power of the Anglo-Irish lords. They did not want Ireland governed by the Irish, and they wanted English control to be a great deal stronger. In the 1530s the Reformation of the Church in England made the situation in Ireland even more difficult. The Irish lords would not convert to Protestantism and their local power and distance from London gave them confidence. This was dangerous because Ireland could become a 'back door' for a foreign invasion of England.

b) Wales

Wales was another area where there was lawlessness. It was especially difficult for the King's council in Wales to stop lawlessness because it lacked soldiers to capture criminals in the ruged terrain and the Welsh kept their own laws and language.

c) The north of England

The north (all the land north of the River Trent, including Lancashire, Yorkshire, Cumbria and Northumbria) was governed by the Council of the North, a special council based in York. However, the northern nobility also had great power and the King depended on them to maintain law and order.

The Pilgrimage of Grace, the great rebellion of 1536, revealed a serious problem in the north. Many people there were strongly Catholic. Incensed by Henry's Dissolution of the Monasteries, they rebelled to protect their faith. The local nobility and officials were slow to act to stop the rising, partly because some sympathised with the rebels, and so the danger from the Pilgrimage increased.

Cromwell and Henry managed to restore order but it was the most serious threat to Henry's monarchy during his reign. Something needed to be done to reinforce the authority of the Crown and speed up the reaction time of Henry's northern officials.

▲ Map of Ireland showing the Pale.

Cromwell's solutions

a. Ireland: A permanent military force was established in the Pale so the English Lord Deputy did not have to rely on the Anglo-Irish lords for military help. However, Cromwell did not try to extend English control beyond the Pale because of the costs and risks.

b. Wales: In 1536 an Act of Union said that English laws replaced Welsh laws. Wales was divided into counties which sent MPs to the English Parliament and English became the official language of government throughout Wales. This completed the English take-over of Wales.

c. The north of England: Cromwell reorganised the Council of the North and gave it greater responsibility for law and order – dealing with serious crimes like rape, murder and treason. This improved royal security in the north, but northern lords remained extremely powerful and the Crown was still dependent on their loyalty and goodwill to maintain law and order.

ROYAL POWER

1. Complete your table from page 63, collecting evidence for Cromwell's effectiveness and reaching your judgement.

2. Look back to Decision 2 on page 62. Did Cromwell choose one of the options – or something different?

Royal finance

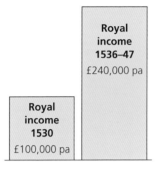

▲ The increase in royal income 1530–1547

It was particularly important for Henry VIII to maximise his income in the 1530s. He needed to show off his power by keeping a magnificent Court and used his 'ordinary revenue' (see page 25) for this, which included money from rents paid by farmers, fines from law courts and taxes on trade and the Church. In addition, the danger of invasion by Catholic countries meant more money was needed to cover the costs of defence.

In the 1530s Henry received a windfall that would never be repeated – the income from the Dissolution of the Monasteries, raised by selling off the monastic lands and by confiscating an enormous amount of gold and silver ornaments from churches. Cromwell had to make sure that this income was as great as possible.

He succeeded. In 1530 Henry's income had been about £100,000 per year. Between 1536 and his death in 1547, Henry's income was about £240,000 per year, enough to enable him to build new warships like the *Mary Rose*.

Cromwell's solutions

1. He established a special court, the Court of Augmentations, to handle the money from the Dissolution of the Monasteries with a central staff and regional officers to make sure the maximum income was obtained.

2. Many lands were sold off quickly to noblemen, raising large sums of money for the king.

3. When a landowner died and his heir was still a child, the Crown looked after the estate until the new heir came of age. Cromwell established a new Court of Wards to ensure that some of their income went to the King.

ROYAL FINANCE ?

1. Complete your table from page 63, collecting evidence for Cromwell's effectiveness and reaching your judgement.

2. Look back to Decision 3 on page 62. Did Cromwell choose one of the options – or something different?

Parliament

At the beginning of Henry's reign, Parliament was only called occasionally to raise money for wars or approve new laws. As the timeline shows, years could pass with no parliaments at all. In the 1530s this changed dramatically because Henry and Cromwell needed to call Parliament far more often to pass the laws which changed the country's religion and established the King as the Supreme Head of the Church.

However, there was no point in calling Parliament if members then opposed the laws the King needed to have passed or criticised the King's policies. There was a danger that Parliament could become a centre of opposition to Henry's religious changes instead of showing that there was great support for them.

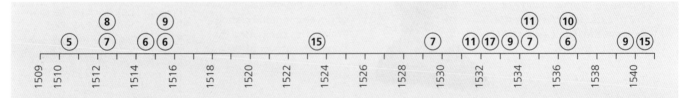

Numbers in circles = no. of weeks Parliament met
In some years there were two sittings of Parliament

▲ This timeline shows how often the King called a meeting of Parliament. Parliament met much more frequently after 1530 to deal with religious changes.

THE HOUSE OF LORDS CHANGED

The Dissolution of the Monasteries removed all the leaders of monastic houses – **abbots** and priors – from the House of Lords. This decreased the political power of the Church and increased the political power of the nobles (known as lay peers). This is how membership of the

House of Lords changed in the 1530s:

1529	1540
51 lay peers (nobles)	50 lay peers
20 bishops	20 bishops
29 abbots and priors	✕

PARLIAMENT

1. Complete your table from page 63, collecting evidence for Cromwell's effectiveness and reaching your judgement.
2. Look back to Decision 4 on page 62. Did Cromwell choose one of the options – or something different?

Cromwell's solutions

1. In 1532 Cromwell and Henry forced the House of Commons to 'divide' (vote) for the first time. This put MPs under pressure to vote for what the King wanted because Henry would know who had supported him.
2. In 1533 Cromwell made sure many new MPs supported the King's reforms. He did this by 'managing' (interfering with) elections with bribery, promise of rewards or by threats. This was not new but it was effective.
3. If members of the House of Lords disagreed with royal policy, they were told by Cromwell that 'they need not attend'. This was a way of keeping disagreement out of the Lords.
4. Cromwell wrote pamphlets outlining new laws for the MPs to read in advance. This propaganda helped to ensure that MPs voted for royal policies.

Thomas Cromwell

Communicating your answer: Did Cromwell make the King's government more effective?

0	1	2	3
Ineffective. Cromwell's reforms failed to achieve any improvement in this area.	Partly effective. Cromwell's reforms made some improvement but left the basic problem unchanged.	Mostly effective. Cromwell's reforms made a big difference to this area of government but did not solve the whole problem.	Very effective. Cromwell's reform of this topic solved the problem the King faced.

The words and phrases on the Word Wall (right) can be used to show how far you agree with a statement in a question like the one above.

1. Work with a partner. Make sure your table from page 63 is complete, then confirm your decisions about where each area goes on the continuum line above.
2. Identify two pieces of evidence which justify your choice of area or areas as being the most effective reform. (If you think two were equally effective identify two pieces of evidence for each.)
3. Identify one piece of evidence to justify where you have placed each of the other areas on the continuum.
4. Look at the Word Wall. Which phrase or phrases best applies to Cromwell's reform of each area?
5. Write a summary of your answer to the question. You can find other questions on this area in the Practice Questions box on page 74.

...was revolutionised in...
...totally changed during...
...was transformed during...
...there was fundamental change in...
The period saw significant/important progress in...
...saw some changes in...
...saw some progress in...
...saw limited/slight/minimal progress in...

6.3 Why was Thomas Cromwell executed in 1540?

▲ A portrait of Thomas Cromwell painted by Hans Holbein around 1532–1534.

Thomas Cromwell achieved a great deal for Henry VIII during the 1530s – finding a way to end his marriage to Catherine of Aragon, setting up the Church of England, dealing with religious opponents and clearing the way for Henry's marriage to Jane Seymour. Henry's government was more efficient and he was wealthier than ever before. Therefore it does not seem surprising that, in April 1540, Henry VIII conferred on Cromwell the title of Earl of Essex. This seems a very fitting reward for such a loyal and effective royal servant. What happened next was not!

Two months later, on 10 June 1540, Cromwell was arrested and taken to the Tower of London. There he was interrogated by the Duke of Norfolk, who accused him of the charges shown below. Norfolk must have enjoyed the experience as much as Cromwell was terrified by it. However, Cromwell used all his legal knowledge and skill to defend himself, always hoping the King would change his mind. Cromwell even continued to work in prison to free the King from his disastrous marriage to Anne of Cleves, a German princess.

THE CHARGES AGAINST CROMWELL

a) Cromwell protected Protestants against charges of heresy.
b) Cromwell had been plotting to marry Mary Tudor, Henry's daughter, who was Catholic.
c) Cromwell had failed to enforce the Act of Six Articles, which turned the country's religion back towards Catholicism.
d) Cromwell was guilty of *constructive treason* – that is, that looking back over his career, it was clear that he had tried to make himself as great as the King.

It is a tribute to Cromwell's skills of argument and persuasion that his enemies did not put him on trial, where his words might influence the judges. Instead, they brought into Parliament a Bill of Attainder, charging Cromwell with treason. In Parliament Cromwell would not get the chance to defend himself. Instead Parliament simply voted to find him guilty or innocent – and they voted for 'Guilty'. It was a technique Cromwell had used himself and he must have known there was no way out.

In desperation he sent one final letter to Henry, on 30 June, ending with a plea that echoes his fear across 450 years:

> Written at the Tower this Wednesday the last of June with the heavy heart and the trembling hand of your highness' most heavy and most miserable prisoner and poor slave Thomas Cromwell.
>
> Most gracious prince I cry for mercy, mercy, mercy!

On 28 July 1540 Cromwell was taken from his cell to his execution. He made a brave speech on the scaffold before kneeling to the block. It was a botched job: the executioner took several blows to sever his head from his body.

Your enquiry: Why was Thomas Cromwell executed in 1540?

Your task is to find out why Cromwell fell from power and was executed. The answers may seem obvious because Cromwell was charged with the offences shown opposite and on the iceberg shown here in the section above the water. However, you know from your work on Anne Boleyn's execution that icebergs conceal more than they show.

CREATING YOUR HYPOTHESIS – THINK BACK AND CONNECT

This is the third enquiry about the downfall of an individual, so in this enquiry on Cromwell's fall you can make a flying start by thinking back to what you learned about Wolsey and Anne Boleyn.

1. Make a list of the reasons which led to Wolsey and Anne losing power. Try to do this without looking back through the book, then check back to see if you are right. This is good revision as well as helping to begin this enquiry.

2. Use your lists and everything you have learned so far about the reign of Henry VIII to decide:
   a) which other reasons might go into the iceberg to explain Cromwell's fall
   b) which reasons you think probably played the greatest part in Cromwell's fall. Use the language on the thermometer to guide you.

3. Draw your own copy of the thermometer and pencil on to it the reasons on the iceberg. You now have a hypothesis to begin your enquiry.

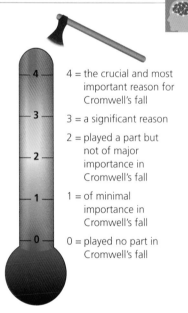

4 = the crucial and most important reason for Cromwell's fall

3 = a significant reason

2 = played a part but not of major importance in Cromwell's fall

1 = of minimal importance in Cromwell's fall

0 = played no part in Cromwell's fall

Visible learning

Using what you know already

One of the most common mistakes students make is to ignore what they already know. They see a new topic such as 'Why was Cromwell executed?' and think they are starting completely from scratch without any useful knowledge or understanding in their minds that can help them get off to a good start. For this topic you already have two different kinds of knowledge:

a) What you have already learned about why Wolsey and Anne Boleyn lost power. The answers may not be exactly the same for Cromwell but there's a good chance they all have some reasons in common.

b) What you know about how to answer a causation question effectively. You know you need to identify several factors, think about whether any are linked together and, perhaps, whether any stand out as being more important than others.

So give yourself some credit with any new topic and begin by identifying what you already know.

Organising your enquiry

Cause:

Evidence of this cause helping to explain Cromwell's fall:

Links to other causes:

Significance in Cromwell's fall:

As this is the third enquiry into the reasons for the fall of a powerful figure at Henry's Court we are increasing the level of challenge this time! We have already asked you to start thinking about possible answers by using your knowledge of earlier events in Henry's reign – that really does make you *think* and not just look for ready-made answers in this chapter.

Now we are going to both help you **and** make the challenge harder. This page helps you to organise your research with two Knowledge Organisers but this is going to be harder as we want you to use both at once as you read pages 71–74! This will make you think harder as you go – not just about individual reasons but also about how they were connected in bringing about Cromwell's fall.

1. Identifying and evaluating the reasons for Cromwell's fall.

Create a card or sheet like the one on the left for each of the causes of Cromwell's fall that you discover on pages 71–74. Fill in as much detail as you can and then use the descriptors on the thermometer on page 69 to complete the Significance section.

2. Identifying the connections between the reasons.

This is another activity you have done before – when you explored the fall of Wolsey on page 42. In that activity we gave you the links and asked you to explain them. This time it's your task to identify the links for yourself, using the text on pages 71–74 to help you.

Draw your own large copy of the chart below, then, as you read:

a) Fill in the boxes with the reasons for Cromwell's fall – there may be more or fewer reasons than the number of boxes shown here!

b) Identify any links between the reasons and draw lines to show those links. Then add notes to the diagram explaining those links. Do this in pencil to begin with so you can re-think and revise the whole diagram when you reach the end of the enquiry.

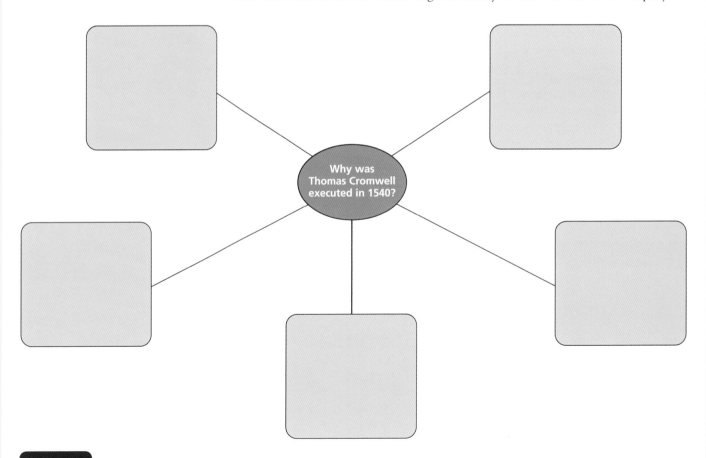

Why was Thomas Cromwell executed in 1540?

Cromwell's fall from power

Remember – as you read each section of pages 71–73, complete the activities set up on page 70. The questions on these pages provide some prompts to think about.

a) Cromwell's ambitions for power

This reason appears in the top section of the iceberg on page 69 because it played a big part in the charges against Cromwell in 1540. It was said that for over ten years Cromwell had been building up his power and wealth, trying to make himself as great as the King. Among the evidence for this was the claim that Cromwell had been planning to marry King Henry's eldest daughter, Mary Tudor, and so become a central member of the royal family. Such ambition, to rival the King in terms of power, was treason.

However this charge was not true! There is no evidence to support either that Cromwell was so ambitious in general or that he had any plans to marry Mary. In fact that is a very strange ambition as Mary, the daughter of Catherine of Aragon, was a devout Catholic and would never marry Cromwell, the man responsible for the break with Rome.

So these were 'trumped-up' charges, false accusations created to win the verdict 'Guilty of Treason' and ensure that Cromwell was executed. However, they do raise important questions – who was behind the charges against Cromwell? Who wanted him to be executed?

> If these charges were false, does that mean they should be taken off the iceberg of reasons completely? Or did they still play a part in Cromwell's fall even though they were false?

b) Cromwell's enemies

We have already met Thomas Howard, Duke of Norfolk. He had been the most powerful figure in the Boleyn faction (see page 40) and had played a leading part in pushing Wolsey from power. It was Norfolk's niece, Anne Boleyn, who then became queen and Norfolk became even more powerful as a result. However, when it became clear that Henry was about to end his marriage to Anne, Norfolk abandoned her to her fate. Norfolk was utterly ruthless in defending his own power.

There were three reasons why Norfolk wanted to see the end of Cromwell as Henry's Chief Minister:

1. Norfolk believed nobles like himself should be the King's advisers, not low-born upstarts such as Wolsey and Cromwell. In June 1539 Norfolk and Cromwell had a public argument about whether Wolsey had been a loyal servant to the King, with Cromwell still loyally standing up for his old master.
2. Without Cromwell, Norfolk would be closer to the King. This would give him a greater chance of rewards and of influencing the King's decisions about religion.
3. Norfolk was a Catholic, deeply opposed to the religious changes promoted by Cromwell. One of Norfolk's closest allies against Cromwell was Stephen Gardiner, the Bishop of Winchester, who helped Norfolk persuade Henry that Cromwell's Reformation of the Church (see page 76) had gone too far.

So Norfolk led the campaign against Cromwell, just as he had against Wolsey. And history was repeating itself in another way – Norfolk had a second niece, Catherine Howard, whom he brought to Court and introduced to Henry. Catherine was 19, pretty and sexually attractive. If Catherine was queen she could help her uncle Norfolk by persuading Henry to get rid of Cromwell – for good.

However, Norfolk's plans did not lead directly to Cromwell's fall because Norfolk and his allies faced the two problems you can see in the diagram on the right. Something had to happen to turn the situation in their favour and destroy Henry's confidence in Cromwell.

> The King has every confidence in Cromwell.

> The King is about to marry a German princess.

> Why did Norfolk need other events to help him get rid of Cromwell?

▲ Anne of Cleves, painted by Hans Holbein. Anne was perhaps the luckiest of Henry's wives. Unlike Catherine of Aragon she accepted the end of her brief marriage and lived comfortably in England until her death in 1557. She learned reasonable English within weeks of her arrival, suggesting intelligence and common sense.

c) The Cleves marriage

The King wanted a wife – and this time he wanted a foreign wife. During the 1530s there were regular 'invasion scares' when Henry and his advisers feared that England was about to be invaded by the great Catholic rulers of Europe. The greatest of the scares came early in 1539 when Francis I and the Emperor Charles V made a peace treaty and the Pope encouraged them to attack England to restore Catholicism.

Henry therefore wanted a wife to seal an alliance with another ruler to make France and the Empire think twice about invading England. Advised by Cromwell, Henry selected Anne of Cleves. Cleves was a small state in Germany and the Duke of Cleves was a Catholic but allied to a league of German Protestants. Cromwell hoped this alliance would put an end to the possibility of invasion.

Henry's advisers did their research on Anne, getting portraits painted and listening to reports of her. Henry naturally made sure he was well informed and finally made the decision himself. 'By God, I trust in no-one but myself,' he said, 'This touches me too near.'

Unfortunately Anne did not live up to her portraits, at least in Henry's eyes. Henry took an immediate dislike to her. 'I like her not! I like her not!' he shouted at Cromwell. If he had known what she was like, he said, 'she should not have come within this realm'.

Henry went ahead with the wedding, though, because of more rumours of invasion after Francis and Charles celebrated New Year 1540 together in Paris. However, the invasion fear quickly disappeared when the peace between Francis and Charles ended. Now free from the need for the Cleves alliance, Henry immediately demanded a divorce from Anne.

For Cromwell, arranging the divorce was easy because the marriage had never been consummated. However, ending the marriage played into the hands of Cromwell's enemies because Henry had already decided on his next wife – Catherine Howard, Norfolk's niece.

If I do not arrange the King's divorce he will be very angry and may dismiss me.

If I do arrange the King's divorce then Norfolk will become more powerful. He and the new queen will try to persuade the King to dismiss me.

Thomas Cromwell

Should invasion fears be in your chart as a separate reason for Cromwell's fall?

Henry was deeply angry with Cromwell for arranging such a humiliating marriage. This seemed to be the opportunity Norfolk and his allies had been waiting for because Henry's confidence in Cromwell had fallen. However, they knew that Henry's moods changed rapidly and if he was happy with Catherine he could well forget his disappointment with Cromwell. Norfolk needed more evidence to push Cromwell over the edge.

d) Religious differences

Religion mattered to Henry. He knew that even kings could suffer the pains of hell if they not had lived according to the Church's laws. He had been a loyal son of the Catholic Church until the need for the annulment led to setting up the Church of England. However, as the diagram below shows, Henry had only ever taken a few steps away from the Catholic religion. He did not agree at all with Protestants who wanted the changes shown on the right of the diagram.

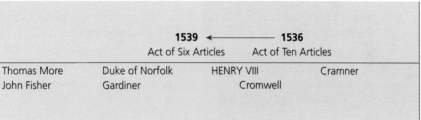

CATHOLIC CHURCH
- led by Pope and bishops
- decorated churches
- belief that bread and wine become body and blood of Christ during Communion service

1539 ← 1536
Act of Six Articles   Act of Ten Articles

| Thomas More | Duke of Norfolk | HENRY VIII | Cramner |
| John Fisher | Gardiner | Cromwell | |

EXTREME PROTESTANT CHURCH
- local leaders, no bishops
- plain churches
- belief that bread and wine do NOT become body and blood of Christ during Communion service

However, as the 1530s continued, Henry had second thoughts about even the few steps he had taken towards Protestantism. In 1539 he supported the Act of Six Articles, which adjusted the country's religion again, moving it back a little towards Catholicism. Henry had decided to end the move towards Protestantism. This was the second opportunity that played into the hands of Norfolk and Gardiner.

In 1540 Cromwell's enemies told Henry that Cromwell was supporting preachers who were opposing the Act of Six Articles and wanted to make the Church more Protestant. They said Cromwell should have been prosecuting these men but instead he was protecting them. Worse, they said Cromwell wanted to make the Church far more Protestant. There was some truth in this – Cromwell had not prosecuted these preachers but he certainly had no plans to change the Church against Henry's wishes. However, the damage was done – Henry flew into another rage. Cromwell, he felt, had been disloyal and was endangering the King's soul.

Cromwell's enemies took their chance – the charges were prepared and Cromwell arrested while Henry felt betrayed by his Chief Minister.

e) Henry's personality

It is probable that by 1540 Henry's health was making him more likely to turn against even such a loyal minister as Cromwell. In 1536 he had an accident during a jousting tournament when his fully armoured horse fell on top of him. Henry was unconscious for two hours and he never fully recovered. His injured leg developed ulcers, which festered and stank and stopped Henry getting any exercise. The handsome, fit king of 1530 became an old, angry tyrant, his waist ballooning from a trim 32 inches to a gross 52 inches. It is at least possible that his marriage to Anne of Cleves was not consummated because Henry was incapable of consummating it.

Henry had always been quick to blame others for his problems. Now he became more unpredictable and his mood swings grew worse. Norfolk and Gardiner could not have persuaded a stronger, more consistent king to turn against Cromwell. However, this cantankerous, quick-to-anger Henry could easily be persuaded to blame Cromwell for his problems – and Cromwell's enemies knew the best way to make Henry angry. They knew that Henry hated disloyalty and they made sure that the 'evidence' showed that Cromwell had been disloyal and, most importantly, disloyal about religion.

Communicating your answer: Why was Thomas Cromwell executed in 1540?

If this topic appears in your exam you could be asked a question that looks like this:

'Henry's marriage to Anne of Cleves was the main reason for the fall and execution of Thomas Cromwell.' How far do you agree? Explain your answer.

This kind of question is asking you to make *your own judgement* about the reasons for Cromwell's fall. You have to remember to do three things:

a) Evaluate the importance of the marriage in Cromwell's fall.
b) Evaluate the importance of other factors.
c) Make a decision about which factor or factors you think played the biggest part in Cromwell's fall.

The tasks below lead you as far as being clear about your argument – your decision about which was the most important factor.

1. Make sure you have completed your Knowledge Organisers on page 70. These should now contain all the information you need to answer this question.
2. Look at the pattern of links between the reasons in your diagram. Does the pattern suggest that one or more factors was most important? If so, how does the pattern show this?
3. Now work with a partner to write a paragraph directly answering the question. As you know from earlier chapters the biggest mistake you can make when writing an answer is starting before you have the answer clear in your mind.
4. Now use the Writing Better History guide on pages 112–22 and your teachers' advice to plan and write your answer.

Remember that you not only need information to write a good answer but you need the right language which helps explain your ideas clearly. We gave you some examples of language to explain the causes of an event on page 42.

Updating your Word Wall

These words and phrases help you answer questions on material in Key Topic 2 in your exam. Therefore you need to understand all of them – can you explain why each could be useful?

sanctuary,   trumped-up   cantankerous

ulcer   heresy   judgement

Attainder   Council of the North   Court of Wards

Act of Six Articles   Court of Augmentations

I totally/entirely/completely/absolutely agree with…

I substantially/fundamentally/strongly agree with…

I agree to a large extent with…

I mainly/mostly agree with…

I agree to some extent with…

I partially/partly agree with…

I only agree with … to a limited/slight extent.

Practice questions

1. Describe two features of:
   a) Cromwell's management and use of Parliament
   b) Henry's marriage to Anne of Cleves
   c) England's government and control of Ireland.
2. Explain why Cromwell made reforms of the government in the 1530s.
3. Explain why Cromwell fell from power in 1540.
4. 'The most important consequence of Cromwell's reforms of government was to the role of Parliament.' How far do you agree? Explain your answer.

Visible learning: Revise and remember

1. Revise the Big Story of this section

Revise Key Topic 2 by telling the story of the events you have studied in Chapters 5 and 6 from the point of view of an individual who lived at the time. Choose from:

The Duke of Norfolk   Thomas Cromwell   Henry VIII   Princess Mary

The first stage of this activity is preparing a plan of what you will include and what attitude your character has to events. When you have completed your plan, compare it with a plan someone else has made for a different historical character – what are the main differences in the stories and viewpoints?

2. Test yourself

For your exam you need to work at making your knowledge stick in your brain. Answer these questions and don't be surprised to see questions from topics earlier in the book.

1. List three of Cromwell's qualities that helped him in his career.	2. What were Cromwell's four main responsibilities as Henry's Chief Minister?	3. Name two events (and their dates) when Wolsey arranged that Henry appeared to be one of the great rulers of Europe.	4. Name Henry's two daughters and their mothers.
5. Give two reasons why Cromwell succeeded where Wolsey had failed in obtaining Henry's annulment.	6. Which parts of Henry's realm were brought under firmer control by Cromwell?	7. What Act of Parliament made Henry the 'Supreme Head of the Church in England' and when did it become law?	8. List three areas of government that Cromwell tried to reform.
9. Name the nieces of the Duke of Norfolk who became wives of Henry VIII.	10. Where did the Amicable Grant Rising break out?	11. Which rulers were threatening to invade England during the 1530s?	12. What did you find hardest to understand in this section? How are you going to help yourself to understand it?

3. Set questions yourself

Work in a group of three. Set five revision questions each on Key Topic 2 – you may wish to take it a chapter at a time, each of you setting questions for each chapter. You should include: true/false questions, multiple choice questions, questions that require brief answers and questions that require longer answers. Then ask each other the questions – and make sure you know the answers!

4. Assessing Henry's success as king

Developing your answer to our overall question '**Was Henry VIII really a great and successful king?**' is another helpful way of revisiting and revising material.

Think back over Chapters 5 and 6. Which of Henry's policies or the events you have studied in these chapters would you place on each side of the set of scales or on the sheet alongside?

A great king who made important and beneficial changes to life in England

A failure as king whose decisions caused many problems and hardship for his people

Evidence or events that lead to other conclusions

The Reformation and its impact, 1529–40

If the title above sounds intimidating, don't worry. This key topic, like all good history, is about individual people, from the 'great' such as Henry VIII to the 'ordinary' people who were not great in wealth or power but showed themselves great in standing up for their beliefs in the face of great threats. The two chapters in this section investigate these topics:

Chapter 7

Why Henry broke away from Rome and how Cromwell enforced the religious changes on the people of England.

What impact the Reformation had on the Church and on the people of England.

Who dared oppose the Reformation and what happened to them.

Chapter 8

Why monasteries and convents were so important to people at the time and why they were closed in the Dissolution.

The impact of the Dissolution – who gained and who lost.

Why people joined the Pilgrimage of Grace and why their rebellion failed.

Taken together these questions will enable you to answer one overall question:

What was the most significant consequence of the break with Rome?

During Chapters 7 and 8 we will come back to this question and develop an answer in stages.

THINK BACK AND CONNECT

This Key Topic!

Pages 71–73

Pages 48–51

This book pages 4–5

Your KS3 work

One of the advantages of this key topic is that you have already studied much of the content. The staircase diagram shows how you are building on steps you have already taken.

Therefore you can approach this section of the book with confidence. Here's a quick set of questions to jog your memory and show you how much you know already. You can check your answers on the pages shown on the staircase.

1. Give two reasons why religion and the local church were so important to people.	2. How would you describe the appearance of parish churches in the 1520s?	3. Give one reason why Henry VIII broke away from the Catholic Church.	4. Name at least one person who opposed the break and what happened to him or her.
5. Which Act said that Henry was the 'Supreme Head of the Church of England'?	6. What was the major event of 1536 that threatened Henry's hold on his throne?	7. Make a list of the effects of the break from Rome in England.	8. Which of these effects do you think was most important?

7 The break with Rome and its impact

7.1 Henry VIII and the Reformation in the 1520s

The Reformation began with a German monk named Martin Luther. In 1517 he began to criticise the Catholic Church. Luther was a Catholic himself but was trying to reform the Church. The Papacy did not accept his criticisms and soon its dispute with Luther escalated. Luther found support from German princes who resented the Pope's authority. These princes defended Luther against the Catholic Church and changed their Churches in line with his ideas. By 1529 people who agreed with Luther were called Protestants because they were protesting about a number of features of the Catholic Church.

The common thread to Luther's criticisms was that he and his followers wanted the Church to return to its simple beginnings in the days of Christ. You can see some of his main criticisms on the right:

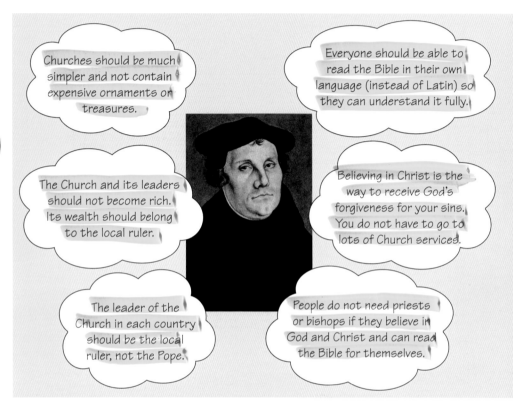

Churches should be much simpler and not contain expensive ornaments or treasures.

Everyone should be able to read the Bible in their own language (instead of Latin) so they can understand it fully.

The Church and its leaders should not become rich. Its wealth should belong to the local ruler.

Believing in Christ is the way to receive God's forgiveness for your sins. You do not have to go to lots of Church services.

The leader of the Church in each country should be the local ruler, not the Pope.

People do not need priests or bishops if they believe in God and Christ and can read the Bible for themselves.

Henry, Defender of the Faith

We know that Henry VIII did not support Luther's ideas because he wrote a book condemning them in 1521. The Pope thanked Henry by awarding him the title *Fidei Defensor*, which means Defender of the Faith. You can still see this title on our coins today, although it is abbreviated to the letters F D. Henry was delighted because it meant that he had a grand Papal title to rival Francis I ('The Most Christian King') and Charles V ('The Catholic King'). Henry had wanted a grand title like this for years and now he had one!

Henry's support for the Pope was not surprising. Henry was a very conservative man as evidenced by his wish to relive the military successes of earlier kings. Henry was very far from being a revolutionary. However, this did not mean that he obeyed the Pope in everything. Henry was a loyal Catholic but believed that in England his power as king was more important than the power of the Pope. 'Kings of England,' he said, 'have never had any superior but God alone.'

HENRY, DEFENDER OF THE FAITH ?

1. What was the core point at the heart of Luther's criticisms of the Catholic Church?
2. What evidence is there from the 1520s that Henry's break with Rome was not inevitable?
3. What percentage chance was there in the early 1520s that Henry would break away from the Catholic Church? (100 per cent = break inevitable, 0 per cent = no chance at all.) Explain your choice.
4. Which of Luther's criticisms of the Church might Henry have approved of and why?

7.2 The reasons for Henry's campaign against the Pope, 1529–33

Henry's campaign – stage 1

Putting pressure on the Pope to annul Henry's marriage

When Henry and Wolsey began their campaign to annul Henry's marriage to Catherine there was no intention to break away from the Catholic Church. Henry was the Defender of the Faith. Wolsey was a Cardinal of the Church (see page 19). They were loyal to the Church and expected that Pope Clement would repay their loyalty by agreeing to annul Henry's marriage to Catherine of Aragon. The three reasons driving Henry's campaign are shown in these illustrations:

▲ Henry was desperate for a male heir but it was highly unlikely that Catherine would have a son. He needed to annul the marriage and marry again.

◀ Henry's conscience was telling him that it had been wrong to marry his brother's widow and that God was punishing him for this.

Anne Boleyn

Duke of Norfolk

◀ Anne Boleyn and her supporters were pushing Henry to end the marriage so Anne could be queen.

Henry's campaign – stage 2

Breaking away from the Catholic Church to end Henry's marriage

The Pope's refusal was a shock so Henry turned to pressure and threats but still did not achieve the annulment. The Pope was under the influence of the Emperor Charles, who opposed the annulment. Wolsey had no chance of gaining the annulment.

Between 1530 and 1532 Henry accepted that a more dramatic solution was needed. This was to break with Rome, create a new Church of England and then have a new Archbishop of Canterbury annul Henry's marriage. By now two other reasons, shown here, were influencing Henry's actions.

HENRY'S CAMPAIGN AGAINST THE POPE ?

1. What is the key difference between stages 1 and 2?
2. Which of these phrases would you use to describe the role each reason in the diagrams played in the break from Rome?

   …was by far the most important reason why…

   The key/crucial/essential factor was…

   …was the main cause of…

   The most influential cause was…

   …played a significant/important/major role in…

   …was of some importance in…

3. Explain why Henry campaigned against the Pope and the Catholic Church in 1529–33.

Anne Boleyn

Thomas Cranmer

Thomas Cromwell

◀ Thomas Cranmer, Anne Boleyn and Thomas Cromwell supported Protestant ideas about reforming the Church.

◀ Henry realised he would increase his power and wealth if he controlled the English Church.

7.3 The key steps in the break with Rome

Pages 80–81 describe the major stages in the break with Rome during the 1530s. You have three tasks to complete using this material.

1. Decide how significant each step described on pages 80–81 was in the break with Rome. You can award each one a mark of between -3 and +5.

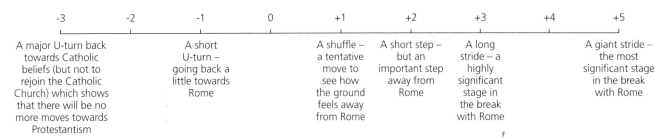

-3	-2	-1	0	+1	+2	+3	+4	+5
A major U-turn back towards Catholic beliefs (but not to rejoin the Catholic Church) which shows that there will be no more moves towards Protestantism		A short U-turn – going back a little towards Rome		A shuffle – a tentative move to see how the ground feels away from Rome	A short step – but an important step away from Rome	A long stride – a highly significant stage in the break with Rome		A giant stride – the most significant stage in the break with Rome

2. Use a large table like this to organise the information you find.

Henry's steps	What changes took place?	How big a step was this? (–3 to +5)	Your reasons for choosing this size of step?
The Submission of the Clergy, 1532			

3. The illustration below shows three routes Henry could have taken once he had decided to break away from the Catholic Church. Use your completed table to decide which of the choices (A, B or C) best represents the route Henry actually took after the break with Rome. Explain why you made this choice.

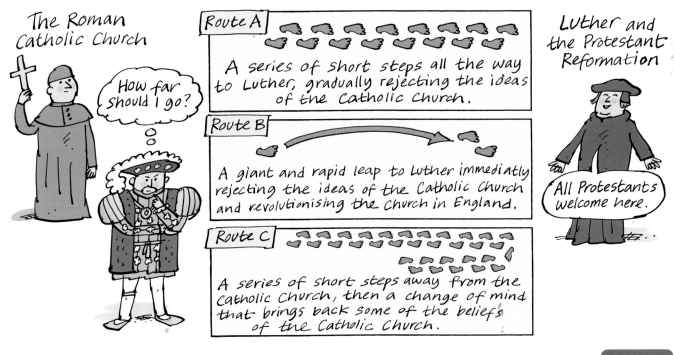

The Roman Catholic Church

How far should I go?

Route A A series of short steps all the way to Luther, gradually rejecting the ideas of the Catholic Church.

Route B A giant and rapid leap to Luther immediatly rejecting the ideas of the Catholic Church and revolutionising the Church in England.

Route C A series of short steps away from the Catholic Church, then a change of mind that brings back some of the beliefs of the Catholic Church.

Luther and the Protestant Reformation

All Protestants welcome here.

Stepping away from Rome, 1532–40

Between 1530 and 1532 Cromwell regularly threatened the leaders of the Church in England with being prosecuted for treason and punished with huge fines. The aim was either to force the Pope to annul Henry's marriage or to make the English clergy ready to accept Henry as the Head of the Church. When the Pope did not annul the marriage Cromwell went ahead with laws that changed the country's religion.

 **1532** **The Submission of the Clergy**

Pressured by Cromwell, the archbishops and bishops agreed in public that the King was their lawmaker. All Church laws had to have his approval. This was the first public step to accepting the King, not the Pope, as master of the Church. Soon afterwards payments of taxes to the Pope by bishops and other clergymen were ended and the clergy accepted that in future the King, not the Pope, would appoint bishops.

 **1533** **The Act in Restraint of Appeals to Rome**

The Church had its own legal system, with the Pope as the final court of appeal. This Act of Parliament restrained (prevented) anyone from appealing to the Pope against a decision made by the King. This shut the Pope out of English affairs and was a second step in cutting priests and monks off from Rome.

 **1534** **The Act of Succession**

This Act declared:

a) The marriage between Henry and Catherine was invalid and their daughter Mary was barred from the succession.

b) Henry's marriage to Anne was his first true marriage, so their daughter Elizabeth was first in line for the throne.

c) It was treason to criticise Henry's marriage to Anne or to deny its legality. Anyone who defended Catherine's marriage to Henry could be executed.

In addition everyone had to take an oath, swearing to accept this Act and so declaring their support for Henry's marriage to Anne.

This Act was intended to avoid the possibility of civil war after Henry's death. If some people supported Mary as heir and others supported Elizabeth, the kingdom would split in two, perhaps into Catholic and Protestant armies.

1534 **The Act of Supremacy**

This Act said the King was now the 'Supreme Head of the Church of England'. All the heads of religious orders had to take an oath recognising the King as the Supreme Head. By doing so, they rejected the Pope's authority in England. Anyone who did not take the oath was a traitor. The oath therefore forced Henry's opponents out into the open so Cromwell could take action against them.

 1534 **The Treason Act**

The Treason Act listed crimes that were treason and were punished by execution. What was particularly important was that the accused did not need to have taken action against the King. Anyone could be convicted of treason simply for saying, for example, that the King or Queen was a **heretic**, for talking about supporting the Pope against the King or saying that the King's religious changes were a sin.

 1536 **The Act for the Dissolution of Lesser Monasteries**

Lesser monasteries were those with an annual income of less than £200 a year. Being small, they were less likely to command sympathy and political support. This was a clever move because it tested people's reactions to closing monasteries without committing the government to closing the more powerful monasteries. Henry believed the monks were still loyal to Rome so closing the monasteries removed a large group of potential opponents.

1536

The Act of Ten Articles

The Catholic Church said that people had to take part in seven sacraments, the seven crucial ceremonies to save their souls from hell. This Act said that only three of the seven really mattered – baptism, the **Eucharist** and doing penance for sins. This was an important move away from Catholic beliefs.

1538 Royal Injunctions to the Clergy

These orders marked the high point of Protestant reform:

■ An English Bible was to be placed in every church. This was a clear move towards Protestantism because Protestants wanted everyone to be able to read the Bible, which they had not been able to do in Latin.

■ Thomas Becket's shrine in Canterbury Cathedral was destroyed (see page 90). This led to the confiscation of money, gold and silver plate and jewellery left by worshippers over the centuries at different shrines to saints. This became known as the 'stripping of the altars'. This was a clear challenge against Catholic beliefs and towards Protestant ones, because it showed that only God and Christ should be worshipped, not saints.

■ Holy relics were to be removed from churches, including all the saints' bones, fragments of clothing, and other objects associated with Catholic saints. This again showed that saints should not be worshipped. Only prayer to God and Christ could save people's souls.

■ All parishes were to keep a parish chest containing a book in which all births, marriages and deaths were recorded.

 1539 The Act of Six Articles

This was a radical shift back towards the beliefs and customs of the Catholic Church. Henry was having second thoughts about how far he wanted religious changes to go. This Act restored several key aspects of Catholic beliefs that had been banned earlier – Mass could be held in private and not just in public, for example. It also banned several Protestant practices, such as priests being allowed to marry. Two bishops with strong Protestant beliefs resigned as a result.

 1539 The Act for the Dissolution of Greater Monasteries

All the remaining monasteries were destroyed, their lands seized and sold, their possessions confiscated by the Crown. This was important because the destruction could not be reversed and, once the land was sold, the people who bought this land had a vested interest in supporting Henry's religious changes.

THOMAS CROMWELL'S INFLUENCE IN ENFORCING CHANGE

Cromwell was the central figure in these events, even though nothing happened without the King's approval. At first, between 1530 and 1532, Cromwell threatened the leaders of the Church with being prosecuted for treason and huge fines. This softened them up for the changes to come. Once Parliament had passed the various Acts, Cromwell enforced them, with the use of oaths being his most important weapon. Many people swore the oaths in church and anyone of importance took the oaths before a magistrate – for example, Members of Parliament, the clergy and officials in the royal government. Cromwell's legal training enabled him to word the oaths precisely so that no one could avoid swearing loyalty to Henry unless they refused to take the oath altogether. Anyone who refused was a traitor. Cromwell then used the treason laws to prosecute and punish anyone who dared to speak out against the King, his marriage and his religion.

THE SEVEN CATHOLIC SACRAMENTS

Being baptised

Taking part in the service known as Mass

Being confirmed as a member of the Church

Doing penance for sins

Priests had to be ordained (welcomed into the Church) by bishops

Being married before living together

Receiving the last rites before death

This box is not one of Henry's steps but explains how risky his decisions might be. In 1538 the Pope excommunicated Henry. This meant he was outlawed from the Catholic Church and could not take part in services that would save his soul. In addition, any Catholic who assassinated Henry would be rewarded by automatic forgiveness of all sins and his soul would reach heaven much faster. For Henry this meant all his Catholic subjects were potential traitors.

THE BREAK WITH ROME ?

1. Explain the significance of the Act of Succession.

2. Explain the significance of the Act of Supremacy.

3. Explain the main features of Cromwell's role in enforcing religious changes.

7.4 Opposition to the Reformation

Route C on page 79 best describes Henry's Reformation. This was not as revolutionary as it could have been but the changes were still very great. Some people refused to accept Henry's Reformation and dared oppose him. Pages 82–84 explore three of these opponents, their actions and how they were punished.

OPPONENTS OF THE REFORMATION

1. Read pages 82–83. Decide which of the punishments listed *you* would have recommended to Henry if you had been Thomas Cromwell. Justify your choice.
2. Then complete columns 2 and 3 of your copy of the table below.

Name	Who was this person?	Why did he or she oppose the Reformation?	How was he or she punished?	Why was he or she punished in this way?
Elizabeth Barton				
John Fisher				
Sir Thomas More				

3. Read page 84, then complete columns 4 and 5 and answer the questions on page 84.

Elizabeth Barton, the 'Nun of Kent'

Elizabeth Barton was 16 years old in 1525 when she had visions of the Virgin Mary, the mother of Christ. Soon many people saw her as a holy messenger who could make prophesies, including the elderly Archbishop of Canterbury, William Warham, who regarded her as a holy visionary, the 'Nun' or 'Holy Maid of Kent'.

When Henry VIII wished to annul his marriage to Catherine of Aragon, Elizabeth denounced the King, saying Henry would die if he married Anne Boleyn. When Henry visited Canterbury, she dared approach the King directly and harangue him about his marriage. In 1533 Elizabeth prophesied that Henry would not last on his throne for another month. She had enough support for there to be plans to publish a book of her prophesies.

PUNISHING ELIZABETH BARTON

How would you punish Elizabeth? Explain your choice, referring to her actions and background to justify your decision.

a) Send her to live in a convent as a nun under close guard and without communication with the world. There she can have as many visions as she likes!

b) Imprison her in a royal castle without any communication with the outside world.

c) Execute her for threatening the King's life and marriage to Queen Anne. She is a dangerous rallying point for opponents of religious change.

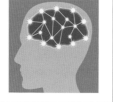

John Fisher, Bishop of Rochester

▲ John Fisher, Bishop of Rochester, painted by Hans Holbein. Born around 1469, Fisher was in his sixties by the early 1530s.

Bishop Fisher was highly respected throughout Europe. He had been chaplain (personal priest) to King Henry's grandmother for many years and had led the service at the funeral of King Henry's father (Henry VII). As the conflict between Henry and the papacy deepened, both sides sought his support. He was the sort of man who others followed.

Despite his years as an adviser to King Henry, Fisher decided to support Catherine of Aragon and the Pope who, he said, received his powers and authority directly from God. The government tried to silence him, but he continued to speak out against Henry's divorce and the transfer of power from the Pope to the King.

By 1532 Fisher was seriously ill but continued to lead opposition in the Church to the King's plans. Unsurprisingly he refused to take the Oath of Succession in 1534, therefore denying the legality of Henry's marriage to Anne Boleyn.

PUNISHING JOHN FISHER

How would you punish Bishop Fisher? Explain your choice, referring to his actions and background to justify your decision.

a) Send him to live his last few weeks or months in a monastery, out of contact with other people. He deserves mercy after his long service to the King's family.

b) Imprison him in a royal castle for the last weeks of his life.

c) Execute him to show that no one can oppose the King and escape punishment.

Sir Thomas More

More was a scholar of international renown and the author of *Utopia*, a vision of a perfect society on a small island. Like his friend, Erasmus of Rotterdam, More had been very critical of the Catholic Church before Luther attacked it. However, More reacted strongly against Luther's ideas, seeing them as a threat to the unity of the Church.

More was also an exceptional lawyer and administrator, Speaker of the House of Commons and a close adviser to King Henry. When Cardinal Wolsey fell from power in 1529, Henry appointed More as Chancellor. Henry knew that More opposed his plans to divorce Catherine but at that stage there was still a chance the Pope might grant an annulment.

Soon More's religious beliefs clashed with Henry's challenge to Rome. In 1530 he refused to sign a letter asking the Pope to annul Henry's marriage and in 1532, following the Submission of the Clergy (see page 80), he asked the King to relieve him of his Chancellorship. The King granted his request, appointing Cromwell as Chancellor.

More retired to his home, where his family was famous for its learning, charity and hospitality. He said nothing about the King's divorce, nor about the break with Rome. However, the Act of Succession required More to swear the oath accepting Henry's marriage to Anne. More refused to take the oath, but remained silent about his reasons for refusal, which made it impossible to prosecute him under the new Treason Act (see page 80).

▲ Sir Thomas More, by Hans Holbein. Painted in 1527, it shows More wearing a Tudor rose on his chain collar. More was born in 1478 so was well over 50 years old by the mid-1530s.

PUNISHING THOMAS MORE

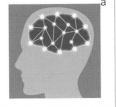

How would you punish Thomas More? Explain your choice, referring to his actions and background to justify your decision.

a) Sentence More to house arrest so long as he does not communicate with anyone outside his family. This punishment recognises his long and loyal service to the King.

b) Imprison him for life in a royal castle, out of communication with the world.

c) Execute him to show that everyone must take the Oath of Succession and that no one can oppose the King and escape punishment.

The fate of the opponents of the Reformation

Elizabeth Barton

Barton was accused of high treason in Parliament and sentenced to death, along with five followers. In April 1534 she was executed. On the same day the people of London were required to take the Oath of Succession, so these executions were clearly a warning to those who opposed the King's reforms. Elizabeth seems to have been an intelligent, courageous and charismatic woman. To some people she was genuinely holy, but Cromwell decided she had to be punished for defying the King and because she had become a rallying point for opponents of the divorce.

Bishop John Fisher

Fisher was so determined to oppose Henry that he refused to take the Oath of Supremacy as well as the Oath of Succession. Even then Henry was reluctant to execute Fisher. However, the Pope inadvertently pushed Henry into the decision by making Fisher a cardinal, one of the highest honours in the Catholic Church. The Pope thought this would stop Henry executing Fisher but it did the opposite. Henry was enraged and personally ordered the execution of the sick and dying bishop.

John Fisher

In June 1535 Cardinal Fisher was executed. However, it would have happened earlier if Henry had discovered that Fisher had contacted Emperor Charles V to ask him to invade England to safeguard the Catholic Church and protect the Emperor's aunt, Catherine of Aragon.

Sir Thomas More

On page 13 we included a comment by More that if King Henry 'could win a castle in France by cutting my head off then my head would be sure to go'. More was all too accurate. He was executed in July 1535.

Sir Thomas More

His refusal to say anything about the King made it difficult to accuse him of treason. However, More was visited in prison by Richard Riche, the Solicitor-General, who testified at More's trial that he had spoken treasonable words by denying the King's supremacy. Riche's testimony was unsupported and possibly made up, but More was found guilty and sentenced to death.

More's opposition had been highly significant, showing that even one of the King's closest advisers disagreed with the reform of the Church. Henry and Cromwell could not afford to let More live as this would have given others the courage to oppose the King. The news of More's execution shocked people all round Europe, but the execution had sent a clear message that no opponent would escape punishment, even a man whom the King had greatly admired.

MORE'S BELIEFS

At the end of his trial, More threw caution to the winds and spoke his mind:

> Seeing that you are determined to condemn me (God knows how), I will now in discharge of my conscience, speak my mind plainly and freely. For as, my Lord, this accusation is grounded upon an Act of Parliament directly repugnant to the laws of God and his Holy Church, the supreme government of which no temporal prince may presume by any law to take upon him, as rightfully belonging to the See of Rome, a spiritual pre-eminence by the mouth of our Saviour himself, personally present upon the earth, only to St Peter and his successors... No more might this realm of England refuse obedience to the See of Rome than might a child refuse obedience to his own natural father.

OPPOSITION TO THE REFORMATION ?

1. Explain why Barton, Fisher and More were executed.

2. How do these cases show the importance of the Oaths of Succession and Supremacy in dealing with opponents of the Reformation?

Preventing opposition

King Henry sitting in splendour presenting the Bible to Cranmer (left) and Cromwell (right)

Henry kneels before Christ to receive the Word of God

A priest receives the Bible from a bishop

The people shout out as they listen to the words of the new Bible

A priest reads from the new Bible to the people

▲ The title page of The Great Bible of 1539. It was the first Bible in English to be authorised by the King's government. All parish churches were ordered to purchase a copy.

PREVENTING OPPOSITION

1. What does this illustration tell people about King Henry?
2. Who are the King's chief supporters?
3. What do you think the people are shouting out?
4. Why are the people grateful to King Henry?
5. Why could this illustration be effective propaganda and reduce opposition to Henry's reforms?
6. What else can you learn from this illustration about any aspect of life at the time?

7.5 Your enquiry: What was the most significant consequence of the break with Rome?

We introduced this question at the beginning of this section on page 76. The question runs throughout Chapters 7 and 8, although later on we will pick out particular consequences for you to discuss. However, you now know enough to begin thinking about possible answers. The tug of war illustration below will help you summarise the evidence 'on the one hand' and 'on the other hand'.

1. Historian A (on the left) has a clear hypothesis. What evidence could you add to the bubbles for the people supporting his argument? Write one entry for each person, continuing from the historian's connective 'This meant that…'. Use the following clues to help you and think back to earlier parts of this chapter.

   taxes   courts   bishops   royal power   oaths (and what, in turn, did oaths lead to?)

On pages 88–89 you are going to begin looking at evidence which might support the view of Historian B (on the right) in the tug of war. This first section of evidence is about changes and continuities in everyday religious life, the kinds of effects that were seen by and affected everyone who went to church.

2. Look back to page 77 to Luther's criticisms of the Catholic Church. What changes do these criticisms suggest might take place in English churches after the break with Rome? Use the information about Catholic churches on page 9 to help you.

3. Read pages 88–89 then fill in this table to identify changes and continuities in churches and in how people worshipped God. Use the Word Wall on page 67 to provide ideas for completing column 3.

	Catholic churches – before Henry's break from Rome	Changes that took place by 1540	Continuities during the 1530s despite the break from Rome	How great were the changes?
What services and ceremonies took place and how were they carried out?				
What did churches look like inside?				
How did people believe their souls would get to heaven?				

I disagree. Other consequences were more important because they affected more people, for example ordinary villagers. It led to.....

Historian B

7.6 The impact of the Reformation on the English Church

Holy days and Saints' days

In 1530...

There were many special ceremonies on holy days (e.g. Christmas and Easter) and on many saints' days, when no work was done.

What had changed by 1540?

Holy days and saints' days were abolished. This had a major impact on social life in English villages.

Links to the farming year

In 1530...

Some ceremonies were linked to important stages in the farming year, such as celebrating harvest and blessing the plough in January.

What had changed by 1540?

Church ceremonies became more detached from the working year, and more focused on rituals linked directly to the Bible.

ceiling decorated to represent 'the heavens'

stained glass windows showing stories from the Bible

bright colours

altar

massbook

pictures of saints

alcove for storing the consecrated bread and wine – the body and blood of Jesus

gold

chalice

priest

server

rushes on floor

rood screen

▲ Artist's impression of a typical church in 1530

What happened during the Mass?

In 1530...

The most important weekly service was Mass which was conducted in Latin. The priest blessed the bread and wine in a ceremony that was believed to be a miracle, transforming the bread and wine into the actual body and blood of Christ. This belief was called transubstantiation.

What had changed by 1540?

The Catholic Latin Mass was replaced by religious services in English, but people still believed that a miracle took place during the Mass with the bread and wine being transformed into the actual body and blood of Christ.

Statues of saints

In 1530...

Churches contained many statues dedicated to the Virgin Mary, Jesus and a range of saints.

Statues were lit by candlelight, illuminating them in the darkness. People believed saints influenced their daily lives, helping them through sickness, harvest failure and death.

What had changed by 1540?

Many of the statues in churches were removed, to focus attention on the Word of God – the Bible – and the sermons given by the priest.

Candles were removed from statues and images, leaving only enough to adorn the church during divine service.

All the ornaments that had been hung about the statue of the Virgin Mary were removed.

Confessing sins

In 1530...

People confessed their sins to their priest, who told them they must show their sorrow by doing penance, i.e. proving their sorrow by saying prayers, performing good deeds, giving to charity, or going on pilgrimage. In return God would forgive their sins.

What had changed by 1540?

People were encouraged to believe that faith in God was more important than confession to a priest, doing penance and receiving absolution from the Church.

Holy relics and pilgrimages

In 1530...

People's souls would reach heaven more quickly if they made pilgrimages to the shrines of saints, such as to Saint Sidwell in Exeter Cathedral or Saint Thomas Becket at Canterbury, or to see holy relics such as a fragment of the original cross or the blood of the Virgin Mary at Hailes Abbey.

The souls of the dead reached heaven more quickly if people prayed for those souls: the more prayers, the faster the journey to heaven.

What had changed by 1540?

Pilgrimages were discouraged and holy relics were removed or destroyed. People were told that their souls would benefit more from giving charity to the poor than from worshipping relics.

Reading the Bible

In 1530...

The Bible and services such as the Mass were in Latin, which most people did not understand. Mass was performed in the candle-lit sanctuary beyond the screen that separated the priest from the people in the church.

What had changed by 1540?

The Latin Bible in Church was replaced by an English Bible – the Great Bible of 1539.

All clergy were ordered to preach a sermon four times a year urging their parishioners to read the gospels and to perform acts of charity, mercy and faith, instead of 'superstitious' practices.

Clergy were required to preach the Royal Supremacy over the Church.

Parents were instructed to teach their children and servants the Lord's Prayer, the Apostles' Creed and the Ten Commandments.

Use the text and the illustration to complete your table on page 87.

7.7 The work of Thomas Cranmer and Thomas Cromwell

▲ Thomas Cranmer, Archbishop of Canterbury from 1532 to 1555, by Gerlach Fliche. When Cromwell fell from power in 1540, Cranmer showed his bravery by pleading with the King to spare Cromwell's life.

Thomas Cranmer initially won Henry's confidence by collecting evidence to show that Henry's marriage to Catherine was invalid. Appointed Archbishop, Cranmer then declared the marriage illegal and led the service at which Henry and Anne were married. As Archbishop, Cranmer wanted to move the Church well away from Catholic beliefs and urged Henry to adopt Protestant ideas. Cranmer was the religious thinker; Cromwell (another highly intelligent supporter of Protestant ideas) was the man who worked out how to make changes happen and how to enforce them.

The main aim of the two men was to get rid of superstitious beliefs and religious practices, especially what they saw as worship of saints, statues and holy relics rather than of God and Christ. This, in turn, meant ending pilgrimages to places where people seemed to be worshipping saints and relics.

In 1538 Cromwell and Cranmer masterminded the Royal Injunctions to the Clergy (see page 81), ordering the end of pilgrimages. In 1538, Thomas Becket's shrine in Canterbury Cathedral was torn down, the treasures, gold and jewels at the shrine were taken by the crown and Becket's bones were dug up and burnt. This pattern was followed wherever saints were buried and pilgrimages took place.

Cromwell was highly influential because, in 1535, Henry appointed him as Vice-Gerent in Spirituals, which meant Cromwell was the King's deputy in everything to do with religion. This shows how far Henry trusted Cromwell because he had given him almost complete power over the Church.

Cromwell wanted to see the Church move towards Protestantism, although he was not as strong a supporter of Protestant ideas as Cranmer. He did, however, pay out of his own money for a translation of the Bible into English and for copies to be printed. He organised a survey of the wealth and condition of the Church (known as the *Valor Ecclesiasticus*), gathering evidence to persuade the King to reform the Church. He then sent out documents to individuals and towns explaining why the reforms were badly needed. These documents were printed so more copies could be sent out more quickly. However, Cromwell also had a strong sense of what Henry would and would not accept. Therefore, Cromwell went along with Henry's decision to turn back towards Catholic ideas with the Act of Six Articles in 1539 (see page 73).

THE WORK OF CRANMER AND CROMWELL

1. What post did Cromwell hold which enabled him to influence the Church so greatly?
2. How did Cromwell collect evidence of the condition of the Church?
3. How had Cranmer won King Henry's confidence in the early 1530s?
4. What were the main targets of Cranmer and Cromwell's reforms?
5. What did they do to achieve their aims during the 1530s?

7.8 Continuing your enquiry

Key Topic 3 has been exploring the question 'What was the most significant consequence of the break with Rome?' If you had an examination question on this topic it would not be so general but would ask you to make a judgement about whether one specified consequence was more important than others. Such a question might look like this:

'The main change for the English Church in the years 1534–40 was that it had to accept King Henry as its head.' How far do you agree? Explain your answer.

On pages 86–87 you began recording evidence in support of the statement in the question when you added evidence to the tug of war illustration below. Now follow these steps to add more evidence and think about your answer, but remember you will not write a complete answer until later in Chapter 8.

1. Use your completed table from page 87 to add evidence to your own copy of the tug of war that supports Historian B's view.
2. Pencil on to your tug of war chart any other events or evidence that you have studied before that you think may support Historian B.

3. Look at the continuum line below.
   a) Where do you stand on the line at this stage of your enquiry?
   b) Which pieces of evidence have been most important in helping you make this choice?

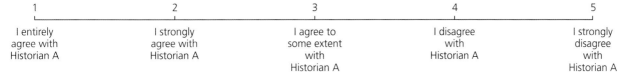

1	2	3	4	5
I entirely agree with Historian A	I strongly agree with Historian A	I agree to some extent with Historian A	I disagree with Historian A	I strongly disagree with Historian A

Updating your Word Wall

Make sure you keep your Word Wall up to date. Here are some useful phrases. What else do you need to add from Chapter 7?

oath   appeals   Supreme Head
Dissolution   shrine   relics
sacraments   prophesies   piety
superstition   pilgrimage   confession
penance   enforcing   visions

Defender of the Faith   Act of Succession
Submission of the Clergy
Act of Supremacy   Royal Injunctions
Act of Six Articles
on the one hand   on the other
to some extent   totally   partially

Practice questions

1. Describe two features of:
   a) The English Church after the Reformation
   b) The Act of Supremacy of 1534
   c) Opposition to the Reformation.
2. Explain why there was opposition to the break with Rome.
3. Explain why Sir Thomas More was executed in 1535.
4. Explain Thomas Cromwell's role in the enforcement of the English Reformation.
5. 'The main reason for Henry's campaign against the Pope and the Catholic Church was his wish to annul his marriage to Catherine of Aragon.' How far do you agree? Explain your answer.

8 The Dissolution of the Monasteries and the Pilgrimage of Grace

Anyone travelling around England and Wales will have seen the remains of a monastery. They are in remote places like the Yorkshire Moors or the Welsh countryside and in the centre of towns, next to cathedrals.

It is often believed that monasteries are in ruins because they are old, but many old buildings are not in ruins – cathedrals, churches, medieval barns and farmhouses. The monasteries are in ruins because they were deliberately torn down. Five hundred years later, it's a miracle that there is anything left at all!

▼ The remains of St Mary's Abbey in York, the richest abbey in the north before 1536. You can see an illustration of St Mary's in the 1520s on pages 94–95.

ASKING QUESTIONS ?

1. How many good historical questions can you ask about the monastery you can see on this page?
2. We have already mentioned the Dissolution of the Monasteries earlier in the book. List at least three things you already know about the Dissolution.

CONTINUING YOUR ENQUIRY

Key Topic 3 explores the consequences of the break from Rome. In Chapter 7 you began building your list of consequences and thinking about which of them was most significant. This chapter continues this enquiry by looking at the Dissolution of the Monasteries and the great protest against religious changes known as the Pilgrimage of Grace, which took place in 1536.

8.1 The role of religious houses in local communities

When you stand and look at a ruined monastery, it can be hard to imagine what it was like *before* it was a ruin. In fact, over 800 religious houses existed before the Reformation. Nearly every town had at least one religious house and there were many more in the countryside.

The main purpose of these religious houses was to provide places where monks could praise God on behalf of all mankind, sending up to heaven a constant stream of prayer. One Benedictine monk described the monasteries as 'castle-guards of Christ, performing a daily round of hymns and prayers. Many of those prayers were for the souls of the dead, because people believed that the more prayers were said for the soul of a person then the faster that soul sped on its path through purgatory to salvation in heaven.

THE MONASTIC IDEAL

Monks and nuns were supposed to live their lives according to the **Rule of St Benedict**, whose ideal focused on three principles:

1. Poverty. Giving up worldly possessions was seen as a way of living a religious life.
2. Chastity. Monks and nuns were 'married to God', so were forbidden to get married or to have sexual relations.
3. Obedience. Monks and nuns were expected to obey their superiors in all things, especially the abbot or abbess who ruled each monastery, and the Pope.

What are 'religious houses'?
Religious houses is a phrase that includes monasteries (where monks lived and prayed) and convents or nunneries (where nuns lived and prayed).

All the kings who Henry VIII most admired – Edward III, Henry V, his own father Henry VII – left vast sums of money for prayers to be said for their souls. In the 1520s everyone assumed that Henry VIII would also leave great sums so that monks and nuns could pray for his soul.

Monks and nuns lived a life of devotion and prayer, their days a strict routine of prayers, services, silences, isolation and work. They were married to God. However, religious houses were great landowners, renting out property to villagers and farmers. They also grew crops on their land themselves and owned vast flocks of sheep. Selling the wool to cloth merchants enriched many monasteries.

How did the monasteries become so wealthy in the first place? During the Middle Ages many kings and noblemen helped to start monasteries by giving them land. St Mary's Abbey, York (pictured on page 94) was founded in the 1070s on land given by Alan the Red, one of William the Conqueror's allies at the Battle of Hastings. Alan got a lot of prestige from this generosity to the Church and a guarantee that the monks would be praying for his soul every day.

Over the centuries many monasteries became very wealthy. However, they remained very involved with their local communities, with the villages and towns around them. Pages 94–95 explore the roles the religious houses played in their communities.

THE RELIGIOUS HOUSES AND THE COMMUNITY ?

1. What was the main purpose of religious houses?
2. How did many monasteries become wealthy?
3. Draw a copy of the table below. Complete column 2 with information from pages 94–95.

Work of monks and nuns	What did they do for their local community?
Providing employment	
Charity to local people	
Providing shrines and places of pilgrimage	
Educating local people	
Preserving Christian culture and knowledge	
Pleasing people with their beauty	

The role of religious houses in local communities: the example of St Mary's Abbey, York

The abbey was the richest in the north and one of the richest is England. Its income of £2000 a year was the same as some noblemen and it ran a school for poor children.

These pages explain the links between the abbey and the people of the city of York.

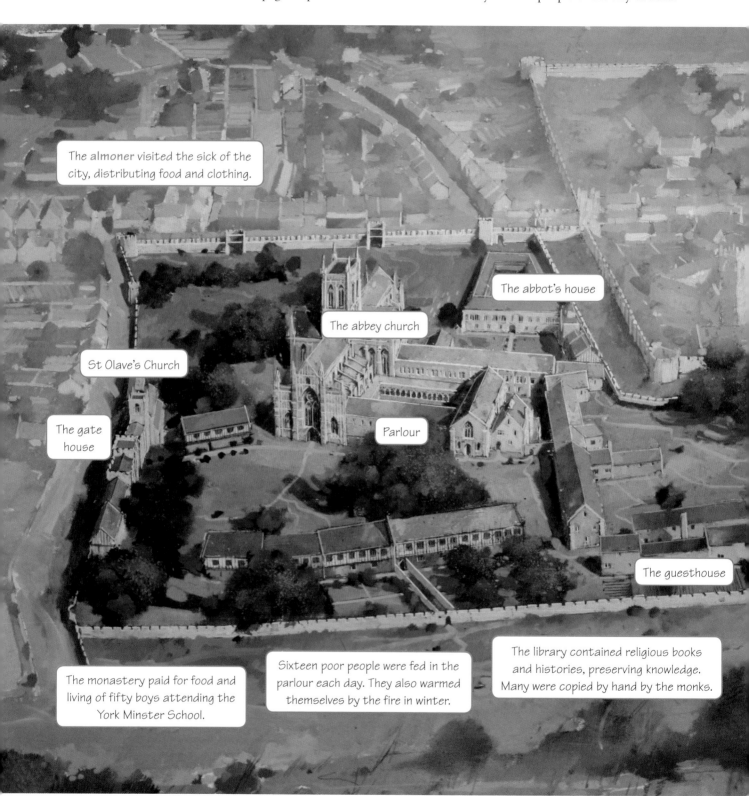

The almoner visited the sick of the city, distributing food and clothing.

The abbot's house

The abbey church

St Olave's Church

The gate house

Parlour

The guesthouse

The monastery paid for food and living of fifty boys attending the York Minster School.

Sixteen poor people were fed in the parlour each day. They also warmed themselves by the fire in winter.

The library contained religious books and histories, preserving knowledge. Many were copied by hand by the monks.

200 local people were employed by the abbey:

1 As servants to clean and cook

2 In the laundry

3 In the bakery and brewery

4 In the guest house

5 In the stables

6 On the abbey farmlands away from York

The abbey bought food from local people, helping them to make a living.

Local merchants made money from selling the abbey rich cloth, and silver and gold ornaments to adorn the altar.

A An extract from a document advising the almoners of monasteries about their duties:

The almoner ought frequently to visit old men who are decrepit, lame and blind or who are confined to their beds, and give them suitable help. Those who in former days have been rich, and have come to poverty, and are perhaps ashamed to sit down among the rest, he will assemble them separately that he may distribute his bounty to them with greater privacy.

B Robert Aske, the leader of the Pilgrimage of Grace in 1536 wrote:

The abbeys in the north parts gave great alms to poor men and laudably served God. By occasion of the suppression, the divine service of almighty God is much diminished. Many of the abbeys were in the mountains and desert places, where the people be rude of condition and not well taught the law of God, and when the abbeys stood the said people had not only worldly refreshing in their bodies but also spiritual refuge... Also the abbeys were one of the beauties of this realm to all men and strangers passing through. Such abbeys as were near the sea were great maintainers of sea walls and dykes.

C Bede, the seventh-century Anglo-Saxon historian, wrote in his book, *A History of the English Church and People*:

I was born on the lands of this monastery, and on reaching seven years of age, I was entrusted by my family first to the most reverend Abbot Benedict and later to Abbot Ceolfrid for my education. I have spent all the remainder of my life in this monastery and devoted myself entirely to the study of the Scriptures... My chief delight has always been in study, teaching and writing.

Pilgrims brought money and gifts to many holy places. Hailes Abbey was one of the most important pilgrimage sites because visitors could see a phial said to contain Christ's blood. The greatest shrine and pilgrimage site in the north was in Durham Cathedral, where St Cuthbert was buried. Cuthbert was an Anglo-Saxon saint who had worked many miracles and was widely praised for his holiness. When his tomb was opened eleven years after his death his body was still as it had been the day he died, therefore proving his holiness. Thousands of pilgrims prayed each year at Cuthbert's shrine, which was richly jewelled and covered in gold and marble. One emerald, given to the Cathedral in 1401, was worth over £3000, the annual income of a duke.

8.2 The reasons for the Dissolutions

Thomas Cromwell prepared the way for the Dissolution very carefully. He knew that there was likely to be opposition to closing the religious houses, not just from the monks and nuns but from many other people too. Part of Cromwell's preparation was to send preachers to churches throughout the country to talk to the people about the religious houses. These preachers were given very precise instructions about what they should say. They had to tell everyone that:

- Monks and nuns were sinful and living in luxury.
- They were taking advantage of working people and giving nothing back to the people.
- The King would never ask the people for taxes again if he took over the wealth of the monasteries.

In 1535 Cromwell also ordered two surveys of the religious houses:

a) A survey to identify exactly what the Church was worth so that when the monasteries were closed he knew exactly how much money the King should receive. This survey is known as the *Valor Ecclesiasticus* (which means 'the value of the Church').

b) He sent inspectors on visitation to the religious houses to investigate the spiritual health of the monks and nuns, which means whether they were living completely religious lives or whether they were breaking their own rules.

The men who carried out the visitations (led by Dr Richard Layton and Thomas Legh) were already working for Cromwell. He sent them off with a list of specific questions, including:

'Whether the divine service was kept up, day and night, in the right hours?'

'Whether the monks kept company with women, within or without the monastery?'

'Whether any monks had any boys lying by them?'

'Whether any of the brethren were incorrigible?'

The results of the visitations showed many problems, but it is highly likely that they were a cynical exercise from the beginning which aimed at finding evidence to justify the Dissolution. Cromwell had already decided to close all the monasteries before the visitations began. When the visitors reported that they had found the monks living a religious life, Cromwell sent them back to have another look! This extract from the report in Maiden Bradley Priory in Wiltshire was written by Dr Richard Layton:

> The holy father has but six children and but one daughter married, yet of the goodness of the monastery, [is] shortly to marry [off] the rest. His sons be tall men waiting upon him and he thanks God [he] never meddled with married women but [always] with maidens, the fairest [that] could be gotten and always married them [off] right well.

Cromwell's visitors also sent him **relics** from shrines that were said to be closely linked to Christ or which created miracles, but which in reality were no such thing. These 'relics' included:

- the phial of Holy Blood from Hailes Abbey, which was found to be water dyed red
- the coals used to roast St Laurence
- St Edmund's fingernail clippings
- St Thomas Becket's penknife
- pieces of the cross on which Christ was crucified.

The range of evidence gathered during the visitations to religious houses was used by Cromwell to justify closing the monasteries, on the grounds that they did not live up to their ideals. The closure took place in two stages. This was probably to make sure that any opposition could be dealt with by the government. It may also have been because King Henry had not yet fully committed himself to closing all the religious houses and needed more time to become used to this huge change in the religious life of the country.

The two stages of the Dissolution were:

1. The Dissolution of the Lesser (smaller) Monasteries in 1536

Parliament passed the first Act of Dissolution, closing the smaller monasteries that were worth less than £200 per year. This Act said that these closures would help reform and improve the remaining monasteries and it actually praised the larger monasteries. Monks transferred to the monasteries that were still open.

2. The second Act of Dissolution of the Monasteries passed by Parliament in 1539, closing all the remaining religious houses

By then many monasteries had already surrendered, effectively closing themselves down and handing over their land and wealth to the King, because of pressure from Cromwell's men.

PREPARING FOR THE DISSOLUTION

1 How did Cromwell try to build support for the dissolution?

2 Why was the *Valor Ecclesiasticus* important to the government?

3 What kinds of evidence did the visitations (a) seek and (b) find?

4 Were the visitations organised by Cromwell objective in their investigations? Provide evidence to support your answer.

5 Why did the Dissolution take place in two stages?

THE REASONS FOR THE DISSOLUTIONS

1. Read these two pages. Identify four critical stages in the Dissolution of the Monasteries and add them and their dates to a diagram like the one below.

2. Draw your own copy of the table below. Complete the table using cards A–H below and the information on page 96.

Reason for Dissolution	Evidence to support	Evaluation – how important was this reason?
Religious motives		
Financial motives		
Political motives		

3. Explain why the Dissolution of the Monasteries took place.

A. Some of the most determined opponents of Henry's break with Rome were abbots and monks. Dissolving the monasteries would silence these opponents.

B. Henry feared that the break with Rome might trigger an invasion by France and the Empire. Closing the monasteries would raise a great deal of money to pay for defence.

C. Cromwell's *Valor Ecclesiasticus* of 1535 revealed that the religious houses were extremely wealthy. If the King had this wealth he could use it to play a more powerful role in European politics. He could also do that without calling Parliament to raise taxes, which was always unpopular.

D. Monasticism is not mentioned in the Bible. Protestants such as Archbishop Cranmer therefore wanted to see the monasteries closed down.

E. Henry believed that the monks and nuns still supported the Pope against the Crown. The idea that a wealthy and influential group of people were loyal to the Pope, not the Crown, was intolerable to Henry.

F. Selling monastic lands to the gentry and nobility would make them part of Henry's religious reform. Even the Duke of Norfolk, who had strong Catholic beliefs, was quick to enrich himself through buying monastery lands and so benefited from the Dissolution.

G. Cromwell's visitations in 1535–36 listed a great deal of evidence that monks and nuns were not living up to the ideals of the religious life.

H. Protestants in Germany and Scandinavia had closed monasteries and so showed that dissolution was possible.

8.3 The impact of the Dissolutions

THE IMPACT OF THE DISSOLUTIONS ?

1. Read through the text on these two pages quickly and list:
   a) the people who benefited from the Dissolution
   b) the people who suffered from the Dissolution.
2. Draw a large version of the table below and fill in column 1 from your two lists. Then complete column 2 with information about how they benefited or suffered.

Winners	How did they benefit?
Losers	How did they lose out?

Did the country look different?

In the years following the Dissolution, parts of the country looked as if they had been sacked by a foreign army. Hundreds of buildings the size of cathedrals lay empty. Twenty years later, the Venetian ambassador wrote, 'on the banks of the river there are many large palaces, making a very fine show, but the city is much disfigured by the ruins of a multitude of churches and monasteries'. Even in the countryside the ruins were very obvious. At Hailes Abbey and many other places, hardly a stone was left visible above ground as people looted the stone to build farm-buildings, new parts on their homes and field walls.

◀ Parts of some monasteries did survive and can still be seen today, such as the **cloisters** of the monastery linked to Durham Cathedral shown here. In Durham and other towns the King allowed people to keep the monastic church for their parish or as the home for their bishop. This explains why the church, cloisters and other buildings survive at Tewkesbury, Gloucester, Canterbury and other places.

What happened to the contents of a monastery?

The King's officers removed everything of value – gold and silver, plates and chalices, crosses and candlesticks, the furniture, the bedding, everything of value. Officials sometimes removed the stained-glass windows, or smashed them out. Catholic statues were destroyed. They removed the lead from the roofs and stripped the buildings of their doors and fittings, leaving them open to the weather. The sheep and other animals on monastic farms were confiscated.

From an artistic point of view, the Dissolution was a catastrophe: 95 per cent of English medieval art was destroyed. Books were taken from the monastic libraries, with some going to the King; other books were bought by nobles, but some were destroyed.

Most monks did better than nuns after the Dissolution. About 8000 monks received small pensions and were able to become priests in the towns and villages. At St Mary's in York the fifty monks each received a pension of between £5 and £10 a year, depending on how long they had been monks, and a small payment to buy new clothes. Nuns, however, could not become priests and could not marry because they had taken a vow of chastity. Their pension was just £2 a year and they usually had to return to their families and hope they would be looked after, though many would not have seen their families for some years.

What happened to the people?

The abbot of St Mary's, William Thornton, did a lot better than his monks. His pension was over £260 a year so he could live extremely comfortably, and he was given land which he rented out to farmers and so earned more money. The abbot of the smaller Kirkstall Abbey near Leeds received a pension of £66 a year, but he was still well off. Pensions were a reward for not opposing the Dissolution. Many opponents paid with their lives. Richard Whiting, abbot of Glastonbury Abbey, was executed (along with two of his monks) for his opposition, although he was nearly 80 years old.

Many people were losers from the Dissolution. The two hundred people who worked at St Mary's in York found it hard to find other jobs because the 1530s were a time of unemployment. The population was increasing so there were more people trying to find work. The poor and sick found it harder to find help, which had been regularly provided by the religious houses.

Monastic schools also closed, reducing the opportunities for education for the children of the poor. Cromwell had hoped that some of the wealth of the monasteries could be spent by the government on education, hospitals, improving roads and helping the poor, but in practice these came a long way behind spending on war and defence. However, some new schools were opened and they had more freedom as they were no longer controlled by the Church.

What happened to the land?

Many people were also angry because the tombs of their family and ancestors in monasteries were demolished. Now there were no monks to pray for the souls of members of their family, many must have thought this was slowing down their relatives' progress to heaven. Local people had also given money to monasteries to pay for gold and silver ornaments and other decorations. All those now belonged to the King, which was never the intention of those who had given them to the Church.

All land and property became the King's. His income more than doubled from around £100,000 to £240,000 a year, as a result. However, the King also sold off half of the monastic land to nobles and gentry to raise cash. The new owners often bought the land for slightly lower prices than normal so they benefited and grew wealthier as a result. This helped to pay for war against France and Scotland in the 1540s and for the castle-building on the coast to ward off invasion by Catholic enemies. This also meant that the King did not have to tax people as heavily, which would have happened if it had not been for the Dissolution.

BEATING THE DISSOLUTION!

It took a very special man to triumph over King Henry and Cromwell. That man was St Cuthbert! When Cromwell's officials arrived at Durham to tear down his shrine they were terrified when they discovered that his tomb held Cuthbert's body looking as fresh as if he had died the day before, not over 800 years earlier. They had intended to remove the bones to stop people worshipping the saint (as they had everywhere else), but dared not remove Cuthbert as his body clearly proved how saintly he had been. The jewels and gold of his shrine were removed but Cuthbert himself was reburied exactly where he had been before. In the 1060s Cuthbert had forced William the Conqueror to flee Durham when he fell sick after doubting that Cuthbert's corpse was so well preserved and in 1346 Cuthbert's body was carried out to inspire a local army who faced a Scots invasion. The Scots were beaten and the north of England saved. It is a great pity that Cuthbert is not the patron saint of England!

8.4 Communicating your answer

Since the beginning of Key Topic 3 we have been exploring the consequences of the Reformation and on page 91 we introduced this question on the theme of consequences:

'The main change for the English Church in the years 1534–40 was that it had to accept King Henry as its head.' How far do you agree? Explain your answer.

On page 86 you recorded evidence in support of Historian A, who agrees with the statement in the question. Now follow these steps to add evidence in support of Historian B, who disagrees, and then decide on your answer to the question.

1. Complete the bubbles on Historian B's side of the argument. In each bubble on your copy of the tug of war diagram write a short answer to one of the questions below:

   How did the English Reformation change:
   a) the appearance of churches?
   b) shrines and pilgrimages?
   c) church services and the Bible?
   d) monasteries and their land?
   e) the lives of monks and nuns?

2. Now you should have a completed tug of war diagram containing evidence supporting the statement in the question (Historian A) and challenging it (Historian B).

   a) It is time to decide whether you agree with Historian A. To make your mind up you need to think carefully about the evidence and use criteria to help your decision. Here are two criteria to think about:
      (i) Which change or changes affected the greatest number of people?
      (ii) Which change or changes most affected the clergy – the bishops, priests, monks and nuns?

   b) Before you can plan or write your answer to the question you need to have your answer very clear in your mind. Decide where on the continuum line you stand and which **two** pieces of evidence best support your view.

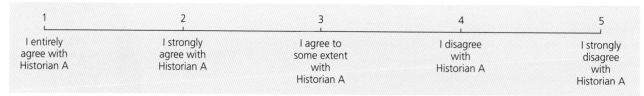

1	2	3	4	5
I entirely agree with Historian A	I strongly agree with Historian A	I agree to some extent with Historian A	I disagree with Historian A	I strongly disagree with Historian A

Updating your Word Wall

In each chapter we have provided words to add to your Word Wall. This time it's up to you to choose the words from this chapter (including from the pages still to come) that you think will help you answer exam questions effectively.

Practice questions

(Some of these questions can only be answered after you complete work on the rest of this chapter.)

1. Describe two features of:
   a) the Dissolution of the Monasteries
   b) the Pilgrimage of Grace.
2. Explain why religious houses were dissolved in the 1530s.
3. Explain why the Pilgrimage of Grace failed in 1536.
4. 'The main consequence of the Dissolution of the Monasteries was that the King became much wealthier.' How far do you agree? Explain your answer.
5. 'The main cause of the Pilgrimage of Grace was the Dissolution of the Monasteries.' How far do you agree? Explain your answer.

8.5 Introducing the Pilgrimage of Grace

WHAT HAPPENED DURING THE PILGRIMAGE OF GRACE? ?

Use the information on cards A–H to complete these activities. The cards are jumbled chronologically so that you have to concentrate to sort out the sequence of events.

1. Create a timeline identifying the main events during the Pilgrimage of Grace.

2. What hypotheses can you suggest using these cards and your knowledge of the 1530s to explain:
   a) why the Pilgrimage started.
   b) why the Pilgrimage failed.

3. What else can you learn from these cards about attitudes, ideas or events in the 1530s?

A. In July 1537, Robert Aske was executed in public in York. Aske was 36 years old, a landowner and lawyer. A few months earlier he had been arrested, then put on trial for treason. He answered the questions at his trial truthfully but was found guilty and then sent north for execution. Before he died he told the crowd that the King had promised him a pardon if he told the truth at his trial. He also said that it was a lie that all northerners were traitors to the King.

B. When the King's officials arrived in the north in 1536 rumours spread rapidly. People said that the King thought there should be no gold and silver ornaments in their churches. It was rumoured that these officials were about to take away those valuables from churches even though they had been bought by local people to praise God, and that the officials would close all monasteries and stop holidays on Saints' Days.

C. What did Aske and his followers want? We can learn a lot from their name and badge. They called themselves pilgrims and their badge showed the wounds Christ received on the cross.

The badge worn by those taking part in the Pilgrimage of Grace.

D. Aske always said he and his followers were loyal to the King and were not traitors. They blamed Thomas Cromwell, not the King, for the problems they were complaining about. Aske said there should be no violence, and stopped his men using violence to force landowners to join them. He made sure his followers paid for all food they took.

E. Between October and December 1536, 30,000 people joined a huge protest called the Pilgrimage of Grace. They came from all over the north and outnumbered three to one the royal army led by the Duke of Norfolk. They took over major towns such as York and Hull and also Pontefract Castle, the largest castle in the north.

F. While negotiating with Aske, the Duke of Norfolk wrote secretly to King Henry, 'Do not pay attention to the promises I have made to these rebels because I shall not keep them.'

G. In January 1537 another small rebellion broke out, giving Henry and Norfolk the excuse to break their promises to Aske. They ordered the arrest of the leaders and many others involved in the Pilgrimage. Between February and July 1537 nearly 200 people were executed. The King said they were rebels and traitors, not protesters following their religious beliefs.

H. In December 1536, Aske made an agreement with the Duke of Norfolk, the commander of the royal army. Norfolk promised the monasteries would not be closed and that Aske's complaints would be discussed in Parliament. All Aske's followers were pardoned of any crimes. The pilgrims went home, believing they had won what they wanted. Aske travelled round the north persuading people to stay peaceful and keep the agreement.

8.6 Explaining the Pilgrimage of Grace

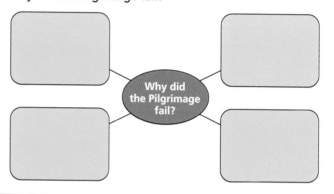

WHY DID THE PILGRIMAGE OF GRACE BEGIN AND WHY DID IT FAIL?

These activities ask you to read pages 102–05 more than once, reading them for different purposes each time. We have increased the level of challenge as you can explore both the reasons for the Pilgrimage beginning and those for its failure at the same time.

1. The first reading aims to add more detail to your timeline from page 101. As you read, add either more events or more detail about events already on your timeline.

2. Now use a pencil to fill in the two Knowledge Organisers on the right with your answers to Question 2 on page 101.

3. Now read these pages again. As you do so, add more information to the two Knowledge Organisers and check whether your initial ideas about the reasons for the Pilgrimage beginning and then failing were correct.

Why did the Pilgrimage begin?

Religious motives	Economic motives	Political motives

Why did the Pilgrimage fail?

Why did the Pilgrimage fail?

The name 'Pilgrimage of Grace'

A 'pilgrimage' is a journey made for religious reasons, usually to a church to pray at a shrine to a saint. 'Grace' means salvation – to enter heaven when you die. Many of the people who joined the 'Pilgrimage of Grace' therefore felt this was a religious event that was important for saving their souls.

The Pilgrimage begins

There were actually three risings in 1536. This diagram shows their relative scale and danger to Henry VIII.

The Lincolnshire rising

The Pilgrimage of Grace

Sir Francis Bigod's revolt

The Lincolnshire rising lasted only ten days in October 1536, but it sparked off the much greater events that followed. Cromwell's commissioners were dissolving the smaller monasteries. Rumours spread rapidly that they were going to seize all the treasures in every church, which meant a great deal to local people. Within a few days it was said that 10,000 people had gathered in Lincoln, led by gentlemen, priests and monks. The fury and fear roused by the commissioners led to violence when some protesters bludgeoned to death one of the Bishop of Lincoln's officials. However, as soon as news spread that the Duke of Suffolk was approaching with a small army, the gentry took fright and asked for pardons. The remaining rebels went home.

The protests, however, were far from over. The news of events in Lincolnshire spread far and wide across the north, inspiring other people to take action. The main event, the Pilgrimage of Grace, began on 4 October 1536 when Robert Aske, a Yorkshire lawyer, called on local people to defend the Catholic Church. Within a week he had 10,000 followers and led them to take over York, the most important city in the north. While in York, Aske wrote down a list of grievances known as the York Articles, which you can see in the scroll below. He sent them to the mayor of York to pass on to the King.

We know very little about Aske other than that he was a lawyer, had only one eye and was deeply religious. You will learn about his abilities as leader as you read on.

The York Articles

1. *We object to the closing of so many monasteries. It has harmed the worship of God, and many poor people can get no relief, to the great hurt of the commonwealth, and many sisters have been left homeless.*

2. *We want you to abolish the Act of Uses, which stops landowners leaving land to their heirs without paying high taxes.*

3. *We want you to change your mind and abandon a new tax on the owners of sheep and cattle. Farmers are too poor to pay it after two years of bad harvests.*

4. *We want you to get rid of counsellors of low birth who are filling their pockets with the people's money, men like Thomas Cromwell and Sir Richard Riche.*

5. *We are grieved that you have promoted bishops like the bishops of Canterbury, Worcester and Lincoln who do not follow the faith of Christ but wish to change the Church.*

Commonwealth

The word 'commonwealth' in point 1 of the York Articles was very important. It means 'the welfare of the people'. Since the 1300s the 'common' people had been very aware of national political events and had taken part in several major, well-planned and organised protests against royal actions that damaged their welfare, such as the so-called Peasants' Revolt of 1381. This Pilgrimage was another such protest.

1. What do the York Articles suggest about the kinds of people involved in the Pilgrimage?
2. Which demands in the York Articles might Henry have granted, and which were never acceptable?

The highpoint of the Pilgrimage

The numbers joining the Pilgrimage rocketed very quickly to between 30,000 and 40,000 people. They arrived in large groups from the areas you can see on the map. They were well organised, using the government's own system for recruiting men in wartime. The leaders were the local leaders in towns and villages, who were used to taking charge in their own communities.

In mid-October Aske led his followers to Pontefract where Lord Darcy (who sympathised with the pilgrims' religious aims) handed over the castle (the strongest in the north) to Aske. The pilgrims now controlled almost the whole of the north and they heavily outnumbered the King's forces. All the pilgrims took an oath of obedience to God and promised to remain peaceful. The King faced a major problem – he had to defend his new role as Supreme Head of the Church so he could not just give in to the pilgrims, but he could not easily or confidently defeat them by force.

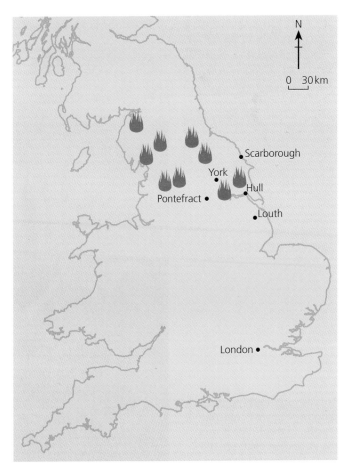

▲ This map of the north shows the areas the pilgrims came from, joining together in bands under Aske's leadership early in October 1536.

The Pontefract Articles

The solution did not emerge for several weeks. In early December the King's representative, the Duke of Norfolk, met Aske and the other leaders of the pilgrims. They gave Norfolk new and more detailed demands, known as the Pontefract Articles, which you can see below. Religion was a central part of their motivation, but so too was fear of poverty and hunger. Poor harvests in 1535 and 1536 had led to food shortages and fear of starvation. Landowners were still enclosing common land (for Wolsey's attempts to reduce this see page 25), making farmworkers unemployed and taking away the common land on which they grazed their animals. Taxation was another problem, because in 1534 Cromwell had begun raising taxes in peacetime. Why did the King need more money if the country was not at war?

The Pontefract Articles

- *To have heresies (extreme Protestant ideas) within this realm ended and heretics burned.*
- *To have the Supreme Head of the Church restored to the Pope in Rome.*
- *That the Lady Mary be made the King's legitimate heir instead of Princess Elizabeth.*
- *To have the suppressed abbeys restored.*
- *To have Cromwell, Richard Riche and the men who investigated the monasteries punished.*

After his meeting with Aske, Norfolk issued a general pardon on 8 December and promised that the abbeys that had been closed would be restored. He also promised that Parliament would discuss the pilgrims' grievances. In private, Norfolk assured Henry that he would not keep any of these promises. The pilgrims seemed to have been happy with the results. They had never blamed the King, but only Cromwell and other advisers. They believed that Cromwell had given the King bad advice and that he and others were milking the country to make money for themselves. They believed they were the 'good guys', trying to save their King from bad advice as well as defending the faith of their ancestors. They set off home believing that Henry VIII was a man of his word. They couldn't have been more wrong.

▶ This seventeenth-century painting shows Pontefract Castle. In the 1530s it was the strongest castle in the north but was taken over by Robert Aske and his followers, a sign of strength of the Pilrimage of Grace.

The end of the pilgrims

Aske certainly trusted the King. He next travelled around the north trying to persuade more gentry to support the pilgrims and reassuring them that he was not a rebel against the King. However, not everyone trusted Henry. A northern landowner, Sir Francis Bigod, believed he could see what was going to happen – after the rebels went home the government would round up the ringleaders, execute them and none of the King's promises would be honoured. In January 1537, Bigod took action. He tried to capture the cities of Hull and Scarborough, but he did not have any support. Bigod fled to Cumberland where he was arrested.

Bigod's revolt played into Henry's hands. It gave him the excuse to accuse the pilgrims of being rebels and traitors and to go back on his promises. The leaders of the Pilgrimage were arrested and put on trial. Aske, Bigod and Lord Darcy were executed, along with the abbots of Fountains and Jervaulx Abbeys. In total, around 180 people were executed. Aske died despite Henry's promises to him that if he spoke truthfully at his trial he would be pardoned. Aske's body was left hanging in chains from the walls of York Castle to deter anyone else from challenging King Henry.

The significance of the Pilgrimage of Grace

This diagram sums up the different ways in which the Pilgrimage was significant.

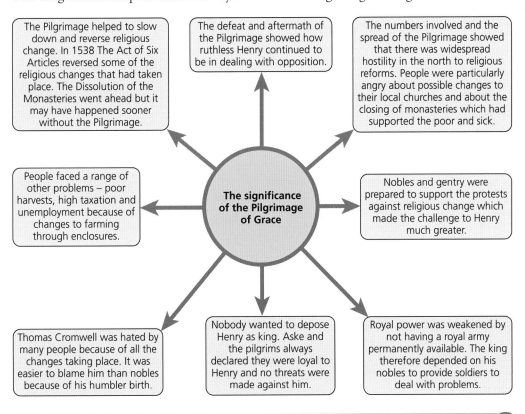

A BALLAD WRITTEN DURING THE PILGRIMAGE

What does this tell you about the aims and targets of the pilgrims?

Alack! Alack!
For the Church's sake
Poor commons awake
For clear it is
The decay of this
How the poor shall miss
No tongue can tell.
For there they had
Both ale and bread
At time of need
And succour great
In all distress

Crom, Cram and Riche
God them amend
And that Aske may
Without delay
Here make a stay
And well to end.

Pilgrims or rebels? What should we call the pilgrims? Most books call Aske and his followers 'rebels', although Aske always said he was not a rebel. To him they were 'Pilgrims' who were loyal to the King, so how could they be rebels? Today we would probably call such people protesters. What do you think they should be called? Why does it matter if they are called protesters or rebels?

THE SIGNIFICANCE OF THE PILGRIMAGE ?

Which items on the diagram above do you think were the most significant telling us about:
a) people's attitudes in the 1530s
b) the consequences of the Pilgrimage
c) the position of the monarchy?

8.7 Communicating your answers

Now you have completed your Knowledge Organisers from page 102 you can plan and write answers to the questions which appeared in the Practice questions box on page 100:

1. **'The main cause of the Pilgrimage of Grace was the Dissolution of the Monasteries.' How far do you agree? Explain your answer.**
2. **Explain why the Pilgrimage of Grace failed in 1536.**

You can find guidance on answering these questions in the box opposite and in the Writing Better History guide on pages 112–22. Also remember to look at the guidance on the language to use for these kinds of question in the Word Walls on pages 42 and 67. Most importantly, always take your teacher's advice as he or she knows your work and what exactly you need to do to improve it.

ANSWERING QUESTIONS ABOUT CAUSES AND CONSEQUENCES

Here are some guidelines you can use to answer these questions on the Pilgrimage of Grace.

- Cover a **range** of causes or consequences – do not spend your whole answer on one.
- **Organise** your answer using categories. For the causation question above you could use factors in the table on page 102. Remember to start a new paragraph for each factor.
- **Prioritise** the causes. Which were the most important? Historians enjoy arguing about the relative importance of different causes.
- **Explain** why you think some causes were more important than others. Prove your claim.

You can use the acronym **ROPE** (**r**ange–**o**rganise–**p**rioritise–**e**xplain) to help you remember these key points.

How important was the Pilgrimage of Grace?

Throughout Key Topic 3 we have been comparing the key consequences of the Reformation. Earlier we focused on whether having King Henry as the Head of the Church was the most important consequence. Now we are going to look at consequences from a different angle by asking this question:

'The Pilgrimage of Grace was the most important consequence of the break with Rome during the 1530s.' How far do you agree? Explain your answer.

On pages 86, 91 and 100 you recorded evidence in support of Historians A and B who disagree about the importance of the consequences. Now follow these steps to add evidence in support of Historian C (on the left) and then decide on your answer to the question.

1. Complete the bubbles on Historian C's side of the argument (on the left), using your work on pages 101–05. Think about:
   - the numbers involved
   - the extent of the danger to Henry
   - the numbers of executions
   - the geographical spread of the Pilgrimage
   - the strength of feeling among the pilgrims
2. Now complete the other side of the tug of war diagram by adding the views of Historians A and B. It's up to you to decide what you think they may believe.
3. Decide where on the continuum line below you stand and which **two** pieces of evidence best support your view.

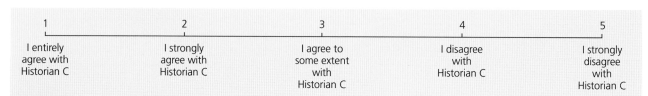

1	2	3	4	5
I entirely agree with Historian C	I strongly agree with Historian C	I agree to some extent with Historian C	I disagree with Historian C	I strongly disagree with Historian C

Visible learning: Revise and remember

1. Remembering the sequence of events

We all have to work hard at remembering the order of what happened in events such as the Pilgrimage of Grace. Nobody remembers the details easily. One helpful technique is to retell the story in a different way. This works effectively because you have to sort out the story in your own mind to turn it into a different format. This is what to do:

1. Break the story of the Pilgrimage down into seven stages (or it could five or six, it's up to you).
2. Choose a headline of at most seven words for each stage and draw or plan an illustration to go with the headline.

This means you have summed up the whole story in under 50 words – but you have a higher chance of remembering the outline because you have had to think through choosing the stages and the headlines and their illustrations.

Which other events could you use this technique for?

2. Test yourself

For your exam you need to work at making your knowledge stick in your brain. The more you think about what you have learned and **especially what you're not sure about**, the more chance you have of succeeding in your exam. So answer these questions and don't be surprised to see questions from topics earlier in the book.

1. Identify two changes to parish churches in the 1530s.	2. Which German monk's criticisms began the Reformation?	3. Identify two things that became law in the Act of Succession of 1533.	4. Who was known as the 'Nun of Kent'?
5. Who was the daughter of Catherine of Aragon?	6. Give three reasons why the Pilgrimage of Grace began.	7. Was the Act of Six Articles of 1539 a move towards or away from Protestantism?	8. What title was given to Henry VIII by the Pope in 1521?
9. List three reasons why the Dissolution caused problems for local communities.	10. Identify three areas of government that Cromwell tried to reform.	11. Name four people executed because of their opposition to the English Reformation.	12. What did you find hardest to understand in this key topic? How are you going to help yourself to understand it?

3. What's the question?

We have provided the answers below but it is your job to come up with suitable matching questions. Try to make each question as detailed as possible so you are using your knowledge to help you word it. This is a valuable way of revising because you have to think carefully about topics from a different angle.

1. Sir Thomas More	2. Robert Aske
3. The Treaty of London	4. *Valor Ecclesiasticus*
5. Anne of Cleves	6. The threat of invasion
7. The Act of Succession	8. 1536
9. Faction	10. The Duke of Norfolk

4. Writing decisions

Planning and writing a set of decisions like those on pages 10–11 forces you to revise the details of events and think carefully about the options people faced at the time. Use the decision-making model on pages 10–11 to write decision activities for at least three of the following:

a) Whether Henry should introduce the Act of Supremacy.
b) How to punish Sir Thomas More.
c) Whether to change the language of the Bible.
d) Whether to dissolve the lesser monasteries.
e) How Henry should respond when he first hears news of the Pilgrimage of Grace.

▲ This portrait shows Henry in the early 1540s when he was a very different figure from the glamorous prince of his early years. The historian J.J. Scarisbrick describes Henry in the 1540s as 'a man of huge girth, eating and drinking prodigiously ... Though he was carried about indoors in a chair and hauled upstairs by machinery he would still heave his vast, pain-racked body into the saddle to indulge his love of riding'.

The year 1540 saw the execution of Thomas Cromwell, Henry VIII's second Chief Minister. Henry did not appoint another Chief Minister during the remainder of his reign though he did marry two more wives. This page summarises those last years, which were as conservative as his early years before the 'King's Great Matter' turned him into an exceedingly unlikely revolutionary.

THE LAST YEARS, 1540–47 ?

Read the summaries of events below, then decide:

1. Which issues between 1540 and 1547 enhanced Henry's reputation and which damaged it?
2. Which of these descriptions best summarises the last years of Henry's reign?
   a) 'A glorious sunset'
   b) 'His best days had gone'
   c) 'An unsuccessful end to an unsuccessful reign'.

War with Scotland – failure

Henry hoped to unite England and Scotland through marrying his son to the young heiress to the Scottish throne. The plan failed. English armies ravaged Scotland in what was known as the 'rough wooing', but only pushed Scotland into a stronger alliance with England's enemy, France.

War with France – more failure

Henry still hoped to win the glory he had always wanted by conquering France. A huge army did invade France in 1544 but apart from capturing the port of Boulogne, it achieved nothing. In 1545 French ships attacked the English coast and Henry's pride and joy, the Mary Rose, sank dramatically without firing a single gun to defend England.

Two more marriages

In 1540 Henry married Catherine Howard, another niece of the Duke of Norfolk. The marriage lasted less than two years before Catherine was executed after committing adultery. In 1543 Henry married Catherine Parr and for the most part they lived amicably together until Henry's death.

Price rises

The costs of the wars with France and Scotland were immense and played a major part in pushing up prices for all kinds of things, including food. Fortunately harvests were consistently good in these years or the high taxes and forced 'loans', which paid for these wars, might have led to rebellion.

Religion

After the upheavals of the 1530s Henry did not wish for more religious change. There were no more major reforms while Henry lived.

Assessing Wolsey and Cromwell

Thomas Wolsey

Thomas Cromwell

Who was more successful – Wolsey or Cromwell? It depends which question we ask. Here are two different questions we can ask about their success:

A. Who was more successful in helping Henry achieve his aims?
B. Who was more successful in improving the government of England?

The cards below show the major policies and actions of Wolsey and Cromwell – though as part of your revision you have to decide which cards relate to each minister (some relate to both!).

1. Focus on Question A above. Award each minister marks for each policy, according to whether it helped Henry achieve his aims (see page 4 for his aims but try to recall them without looking). Use the scale on the line below.
2. Focus on Question B above. Award each minister marks for each policy, according to whether it was successful in improving government. Use the scale on the line below.
3. What were the main similarities and differences between Wolsey and Cromwell? Use your answers to Questions 1 and 2 to help answer this question.

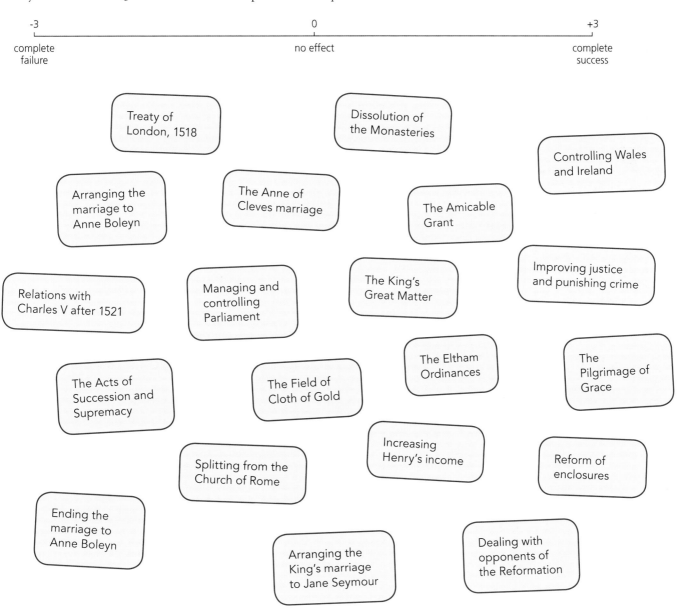

Henry VIII – England's Stalin?

Henry VIII is the most recognised king in English history. A few years ago a cartoon appeared which showed a king visiting a fortune-teller. The caption showed the fortune-teller saying 'You are going to meet a tall, fair stranger. You are going to meet a dark, attractive stranger. You are going to meet a fair, quiet stranger. You are…'

The caption did not need to say who the king was or what the topic was. Everybody knows about Henry and his six wives. So Henry VIII can seem a fun figure, a joker, not someone to think about seriously. However, here is a real story which paints a different picture. It's about the Duke of Norfolk, the duke who arranged for two of his nieces to marry Henry (and watched them both be executed) and who lied to Robert Aske to help Henry end the Pilgrimage of Grace. Norfolk was a great supporter of Henry but in the end Norfolk, too, ended in a prison cell waiting to be taken out for execution.

In 1547 Norfolk and his son were accused of treason and convicted by Parliament. Norfolk's enemies at Court were behind the charges but Henry, by then very seriously ill, agreed to the execution of the duke, one of his oldest and closest supporters. What saved Norfolk was that Henry died first, just hours before Norfolk was due to go to the execution block.

A brutal monarch?

Henry's willingness to execute his own supporters, his friends and even his wives and to order the executions of many other people is why some historians have thought of him as 'England's Stalin'. We know that Henry was closely involved in the decisions about executions because he annotated documents dealing with the decisions and often made sure that the victims suffered as much as possible. When he agreed to the execution of monks from Sawley Abbey he wrote vindictively that they should be 'hanged upon long pieces of timber out of the steeple'.

More people were executed for political reasons in Henry's reign than in any reign of a similar length in English history. This brutal determination to get rid of those who opposed or disappointed him led the historian Professor Sir Geoffrey Elton to write of Henry in the *Independent* newspaper in 1992:

> from first to last he was a dangerous and appalling animal, and the physical decline from splendid adolescence to bloated and sick old age did not signify a similar decline in his character, which was deplorable from the first. Complete selfishness and the ruthless pursuit of private advantage always marked a man who invariably discovered that God and his conscience conveniently backed his desires … only Henry VIII solved all his problems by killing – killing innocent wives and loyal servants – on the simple principle that the best way out of difficulties was to sacrifice scapegoats. The fact that he was handsome in his youth and intelligent all his life should not disguise a horribleness which piled up corpses in his day and problems for a century after.

Of course there was another side to Henry – his interest in jousting, wrestling and other sports, in all things military; his enthusiasm for music and composing songs; his practical jokes and card-playing (like his father, he often lost money to his courtiers!). He was interested in religion but his notes on religious books show what he was really interested in was using religious ceremonies to boost royal power. He even deleted from one book the reference to 'blessed be the poor and the meek'. Henry was not interested in the fate of the poor and meek.

Stalin

Stalin ruled Russia between 1924 and 1953. During that time many of Stalin's political opponents in Russia were executed after 'show-trials' when there was no doubt the verdict would be guilty. Millions of other people who opposed Stalin's policies were executed or imprisoned as he ruthlessly kept hold of power.

Long-term impact

The greatest surprise is that Henry's reign was revolutionary, ending a thousand years of religious loyalty to the Catholic faith. It is surprising because Henry was not a revolutionary. He wanted to be just like other kings before him, charging off to win glory in battle. He did not like change, yet when we look back his reign saw some of the greatest changes in English history – the setting up of the Church of England, the closing of the monasteries, the increasing power of Parliament, England's complete control of Wales. If anyone had predicted such changes when Henry first became king no one would have believed them.

HOW SUCCESSFUL WAS HENRY VIII? ?

On page 4 we introduced the criteria we need to use to decide whether Henry was a successful king. Here are those criteria again to help you reach your final judgement.

1. Did Henry defend his country from foreign threats? (Or did he create those threats?)

2. Did Henry unite his people over religion? (Or did he create religious divisions?)

3. Did Henry help his people live peacefully and prosperously? (Or did his decisions lead to rebellions and greater poverty?)

4. Did Henry make sure he had a clear successor? (Or did he increase fears of civil war breaking out over the crown when he died?)

5. Did Henry win fame and glory for himself?

1. Which criterion or criteria were most important to Henry himself?

2. What evidence supports your choices of criteria?

3. Look at each of the criteria in turn. How successful do you think Henry was in achieving success in each criterion? Did he achieve:
   a) consistent outstanding success?
   b) occasional success?
   c) very little success?
   d) no success at all?

4. How would you describe Henry's overall success as king? Use one of the descriptions on the scales … or write your own short summary.

5. Work with a partner. Your task is to tell the outline story of Henry's reign from 1509 to 1540 in one minute – you can say a lot in one minute! Plan the story using your answers to Questions 1–3 and particularly make sure that your verdict on Henry's success is clear.

A great king who made important and beneficial changes to life in England

A failure as king whose decisions caused many problems and hardship for his people

Evidence or events that lead to other conclusions

Writing better history

Introducing the exam

Simply knowing a lot of content is not enough to achieve a good grade in your GCSE History exam. You need to know how to write effective answers to the questions. Pages 114–22 give you an insight into the exam and provide guidance on how to approach the different questions. This page introduces the structure of Section B (the British depth

study) of your Paper 2 exam. The guidance opposite on page 113 helps you approach your exam with confidence.

Paper 2 is divided into two sections. Section A covers the **period study**. Section B covers the **British depth study**, where you will select:

Option B3: Henry VIII and his ministers 1509–40

Paper 2: Period study and British depth study

1 → **Time**: **1 hour 45 minutes**

Answer all questions from Section A and EITHER Question 4 or Question 5 in Section B.

2 → The marks for each question are shown in brackets.

SECTION B: The British depth study

Option B3: Henry VIII and his ministers 1509–40

3 → Answer Questions 5(a), 5(b) and EITHER 5(c)(i) or 5(c)(ii).

4 →
5 **(a)** Describe **two** features of the Field of Cloth of Gold, 1520. (4 marks)

5 → **(b)** Explain why Cardinal Wolsey fell from power in 1529–30. (12 marks)

6 →
> You may use the following in your answer:
> * the failure of the proceedings in London, 1529
> * the influence of the Boleyns.
>
> You **must** also use information of your own.

7 → Answer EITHER (c)(i) OR (c)(ii)

EITHER

8 → **(c)(i)** 'The Pilgrimage of Grace, 1536, was the main consequence of the Dissolution of the Monasteries.' How far do you agree? Explain your answer. (16 marks)

> You may use the following in your answer:
> * impact on the poor
> * the redistribution of land to the King and nobles.
>
> You **must** also use information of your own.

OR

(c)(ii) 'Thomas Cromwell's arrangement of Henry's marriage to Anne of Cleves was the main reason for Cromwell's fall from power in 1540.' How far do you agree? Explain your answer. (16 marks)

> You may use the following in your answer:
> * the influence of the Duke of Norfolk
> * accusations of treason.
>
> You **must** also use information of your own.

Planning for success

1 TIMING

It is important to time yourself carefully. One hour and 45 minutes sounds a long time but it goes very quickly! Section A (period study) and Section B (depth study) are worth the same number of marks. You should aim to spend the same amount of time on each section. For both the period study and the depth study, it is important to have a time plan and to stick to it.

Look at the plan below. You could use this plan or develop your own and check it with your teacher. We have broken down the depth study into two 25-minute blocks of time. This is because some students spend too long on Questions 5(a) and 5(b), and they then rush Question 5(c). However, the final question is worth the same amount of marks as 5(a) and 5(b) put together.

Section A (period study) Question 1, 2 and 3: approx. 50 minutes

Section B (depth study on Henry VIII and his ministers, 1509–40) Question 5: approx. 50 minutes

Questions 5(a) and 5(b): approx. 25 minutes

EITHER Question 5(c)(i) OR 5(c)(ii): approx. 25 minutes

Checking answers: 5 minutes

2 SPEND TIME DE-CODING QUESTIONS

The marks for each question are shown in brackets. This gives you an idea of how much you need to write, as does the space for your answer on the exam paper. However, do not panic if you do not fill all the space. There will probably be more space than you need and the quality of your answer is more important than how much you write. The most important thing is to keep focused on the question. If you include information that is not relevant to the question you will not gain any marks, no matter how much you write!

Read each question carefully before you to start to answer it. Use the advice on de-coding questions on page 114 to make sure you focus on the question.

3 FOLLOW INSTRUCTIONS CAREFULLY

Read the instructions very carefully. Some students miss questions they need to answer, while others waste time answering more questions than they need. Remember to answer Question 5(a) **and** 5(b). You then need to choose between **EITHER** Question 5(c)(i) **or** 5(c)(ii).

4 THE 'DESCRIBE' QUESTION

The first question on Section B asks you to describe two features of an aspect of the period you have studied. Headings on the exam paper help you write about each feature separately. Advice on how to gain high marks on this type of question is on page 115.

5 THE 'EXPLAIN' QUESTION

The second question tests your ability to write effective explanations. You may be asked to explain why an event or development took place. Pages 116–17 help you write a good answer to this type of question.

6 USING THE STIMULUS MATERIAL

When you attempt Question 5(b) and either Question 5(c)(i) or (c)(ii) you will have bullet points as stimulus material to help plan your answer. You do not have to include them but try to use them to get you thinking and to support your arguments. You must bring in your own knowledge too. If you only use the stimulus material you will not gain high marks for your answer.

7 THINK CAREFULLY ABOUT WHICH QUESTION YOU CHOOSE

When it comes to the choice of final question, do not rush your decision. Think carefully about which question you will do best on. Plan your answer – it is worth 16 marks, half the available marks for Section B of the exam paper.

8 THE 'JUDGEMENT' QUESTION

This question carries the most marks and requires a longer answer that needs careful planning. You will be provided with a statement and you will have to reach a judgement as to how far you agree with that statement. Pages 118–19 provide advice on answering this style of question.

CHECKING THE QUALITY OF YOUR WRITING

Make sure you leave five minutes at the end of the exam to check your answers. If you are short of time check your answer to the final question first as it carries the most marks. Page 119 provides advice on what to focus on. Remember that the accuracy of your spelling, punctuation and grammar is important in all questions as it affects the clarity of your answer.

De-coding exam questions

The examiners are not trying to catch you out: they are giving you a chance to show what you know – and what you can do with what you know. However, you must stick to the question on the exam paper. Staying focused on the question is crucial. Including information that is not relevant or misreading a question and writing about the wrong topic wastes time and gains you no marks.

To stay focused on the question you will need to practise how to 'de-code' questions. This is particularly important for Section B of the exam paper. Follow these **five steps to success**:

Step 1 Read the question a couple of times. Then look at **how many marks** the question is worth. This tells you how much you are expected to write. Do not spend too long on questions worth only a few marks. Remember it is worth planning the 12- and 16-mark questions.

Step 2 Identify the **conceptual focus** of the question. What is the key concept that the question focuses on? Is it asking you to look at:

- the **significance** of a discovery or an individual
- **causation** – the reasons why an event or development happened
- **consequence** – the results of an event or development
- **similarities and differences** between the key features of different periods
- **change** – the extent of change or continuity, progress or stagnation during a period?

Step 3 Spot the **question type**. Are you being asked to:

- **describe** the key features of a period
- **explain** similarities between periods or why something happened
- reach a **judgement** as to how far you agree with a particular statement?

Each question type requires a different approach. Look for key words or phrases that help you work out which approach is needed. The phrase 'How far do you agree?' means you need to weigh the evidence for and against a statement before reaching a balanced judgement. 'Explain why' means that you need to explore a range of reasons why an event happened.

Step 4 Identify the **content focus**. What is the area of content or topic the examiner wants you to focus on?

Step 5 Look carefully at the **date boundaries** of the question. What time period should you cover in your answer? Stick to this carefully or you will waste time writing about events that are not relevant to the question.

Look at the exam question below. At first glance it could appear that this question is about Thomas Cromwell's arrangement of Henry's marriage to Anne of Cleves. This shows the danger of not de-coding a question carefully. If you simply describe how or why Cromwell arranged a marriage between Henry and Anne of Cleves you will not be focusing on the question. If you explain how his arrangement of this marriage made his fall from power more likely, you would gain a few more marks but you are still not focusing on the actual question.

The conceptual focus is causation – you need to reach a judgement on whether Cromwell's arrangement of the King's marriage was the main cause of his fall from power.

The content focus is more than just Cromwell's arrangement of the Cleves marriage. It is exploring a wider theme – the reasons for Cromwell's fall from power.

There are 16 marks available – this means the question requires an extended answer. It is definitely worth planning your answer to this question!

> **5 (c) (ii)** 'Thomas Cromwell's arrangement of Henry's marriage to Anne of Cleves was the main reason for Cromwell's fall from power in 1540.' How far do you agree? Explain your answer. (16)

The phrase 'How far do you agree?' means that this question requires you to reach a judgement about the statement in quotation marks. This means analysing the impact of Cromwell's arrangement of the King's marriage. It also means weighing the importance of this cause of Cromwell's fall from power against other important causes (such as the influence of the Duke of Norfolk).

The dates provided for Cromwell's fall from power are important. The question is asking you to focus on the reasons why Cromwell fell in 1540. If you include references to Henry's later marriage to Catherine Howard you will waste time and not pick up any additional marks.

REMEMBER

It is worth spending time de-coding questions carefully in the exam. It helps you focus on the question and stops you wasting time including information that is not relevant.

Further practice

Look at the other questions in Section B of the exam paper on page 112.

Break each question down into the five steps and check you have de-coded the question effectively.

Describing key features of a period

'Describe' questions only carry 4 marks so it is important to get to the point quickly so you do not waste precious time needed for questions that carry 12 or 16 marks.

Look at the question below.

> Describe **two** features of the Field of Cloth of Gold, 1520. **(4 marks)**
>
> Feature 1: _____
>
> Feature 2: _____

Tip 1: Stay relevant to the question

One major problem with 'Describe' questions is that students write too much! They include details that are not relevant to the question. Make sure you stick to the question – describe two key features of what took place at the Field of Cloth of Gold.

You do not need to:

- include more than two features (extra features will gain you no more marks)
- evaluate or reach a judgement as to whether the Field of Cloth of Gold was a success
- go beyond the date boundaries and describe how the Field of Cloth of Gold affected relations between England and France in the 1520s.

If you write too much you could run out of time later in the exam when you are answering questions that are worth a lot more marks and need longer answers.

Tip 2: Keep it short and simple

You can get 2 marks by simply identifying two features of the Field of Cloth of Gold.

For each feature you identify, add a sentence that gives further detail and develops your answer.

Look at the example below. Then practise your technique by tackling the examples in the exam practice box.

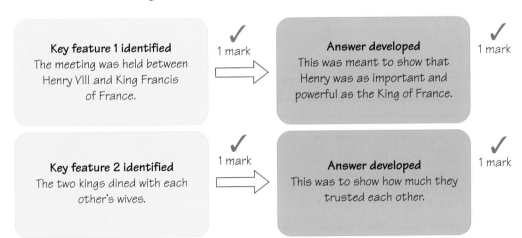

Key feature 1 identified
The meeting was held between Henry VIII and King Francis of France.

✓ 1 mark

Answer developed
This was meant to show that Henry was as important and powerful as the King of France.

✓ 1 mark

Key feature 2 identified
The two kings dined with each other's wives.

✓ 1 mark

Answer developed
This was to show how much they trusted each other.

✓ 1 mark

Practice questions

1. Describe two features of the Pilgrimage of Grace, 1536.
2. Describe two features of Henry's marriage to Catherine of Aragon, 1509.
3. Describe two features of Cardinal Wolsey's financial reforms, 1519–29.
4. Describe two features of Cardinal Wolsey's fall from power, 1529–30.
5. Describe two features of Cromwell's enforcement of the English Reformation.

REMEMBER

Stay focused and keep it short and simple. Four sentences are enough for four marks.

Writing effective explanations: Tackling 12 mark 'explain' questions

Look at the question below.

5(b) Explain why Cardinal Wolsey fell from power in 1529–30. (12 marks)

You may use the following in your answer:
- the failure of the divorce proceedings in London, 1529
- the influence of the Boleyns.

You must also use information of your own.

The conceptual focus is on causation (explaining **why** an event took place). The question is worth 12 marks. The examiner will expect you to give a range of reasons **why** Cardinal Wolsey fell from power in 1529–30.

It is important to spend time planning this question during your exam. Follow the steps below to help you plan effectively and produce a good answer.

Step 1: Get focused on the question

Make sure you de-code the question carefully. Note that the content focus is on Wolsey's fall from power, 1529–30. Do not go into Thomas Cromwell's rise to power as Henry's new Chief Minister over the next five years.

Step 2: Identify a range of factors

Try to cover more than one cause. If your mind goes blank the stimulus bullet points can also help you. For example, in the question above, 'the influence of the Boleyns' should make you remember to analyse the role of Anne Boleyn and her family in influencing Henry and how far they were responsible for Wolsey's fall from power. Remember – you are expected to go beyond the bullet points and bring in your own knowledge – so do not be put off if a factor that you want to write about is not covered by the bullet points provided.

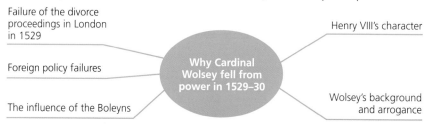

Step 3: Organise your answer using paragraphs

Do not worry about a long introduction. One or two sentences is more than enough and you can use words from the question. Look at the example below. Note how the student has built a short introduction into the first paragraph, which focuses on the role played by the failure of divorce proceedings.

Between 1515 and 1529 Cardinal Wolsey was Henry VIII's Chief Minister but in 1529–30 he was forced to surrender his palaces and the office of Chancellor, charged with praemunire and accused of treason. One important reason for his fall from power was the failure of divorce proceedings in London in 1529. This meant he lost Henry's confidence.

Aim to start a new paragraph each time you move on to a new factor that caused change. Signpost your argument at the start of the paragraph. For example, you could start your next paragraph like this:

Henry's character also played a part in Wolsey's downfall. For example…

Step 4: Do not 'say' that a factor was important – PROVE it was

Remember that a list of reasons for Wolsey's fall from power will not get you a high level mark. You need to **prove** your case for each factor. This means developing your explanation by adding supporting information and specific examples (killer evidence).

This is where your work on connectives will come in useful. Look again at the advice on page 37 and remember to tie what you know to the question by using connectives such as 'this meant that', 'this led to' and 'this resulted in'. For example, you may want to build on the opening to your first paragraph by proving that the failure of the divorce proceedings in London in 1529 was a key turning point:

Wolsey's failure to ensure that the divorce proceedings in London in 1529 granted an annulment of Henry's marriage to Catherine of Aragon angered Henry because he believed Wolsey might have succeeded if he had handled the problem differently. By allowing the matter to be referred to Rome, the decision about Henry's marriage was being handed to a foreign power. It also supported Henry's belief that God was punishing him for his marriage to Catherine. Henry was by now convinced that his marriage to Catherine was a sin in the eyes of God and had to be annulled.

Step 5: End your answer with a thoughtful conclusion

Keep your conclusion short. A good conclusion makes the overall argument clear – it is not a detailed summary of everything you have already written! Make it clear which factor played the most important role. You may want to show how it links to other factors.

Advice	**Model**
Start by showing that you are aware that a range of factors played a role.	Cardinal Wolsey had succeeded for many years in preventing noble factions at Court from developing and challenging his authority.
Make it clear which factor you think played the most important role.	However, the potential for such factions was always there. Wolsey's failure to persuade the Pope to annul Henry's marriage to Catherine weakened his influence with Henry and gave the Boleyn faction the opportunity to undermine his position.
Support your argument with your key reason why you have come to this conclusion.	As Wolsey's influence grew weaker, Henry's character became a decisive factor. Henry was no longer the young, inexperienced king who had relied on Wolsey's advice. When Wolsey appealed to foreign rulers for help, Henry's patience finally snapped and Wolsey was accused of high treason.

Practice questions

You can find further 'explain' practice questions on pages 30, 43, 59, 74, 91 and 100.

REMEMBER

Do not try to cover too many reasons for an event. Select those causes you can make the strongest argument for. Remember in the exam you will have approximately 15 minutes to answer this question.

Making judgements – tackling the 16-mark question

The last question on the exam paper carries the most marks and requires a carefully planned, detailed answer. You will be provided with a statement in quotation marks and be asked to reach a judgement about **how far you agree** with it. The phrase 'how far' is important as it is unlikely that you will totally agree or disagree with the statement. The examiner will be looking for you to show that you can weigh the evidence for and against the statement.

Look at the example below.

> **(c)(i)** 'The Pilgrimage of Grace, 1536, was the main consequence of the Dissolution of the Monasteries.' How far do you agree? Explain your answer. (16 marks)
>
> You may use the following in your answer:
> • impact on the poor
> • the redistribution of land to the King and nobles.
>
> **You must** also use information of your own.

Follow the same steps that you would for an 'explain' question (see page 116).

Step 1: Focus

The content focus is important – you have to reach a judgement on the main consequence of the Dissolution of the Monasteries. The conceptual focus is on consequences. Focus on the phrase 'main consequence' in the question – do you think the Pilgrimage of Grace was 'the main consequence' of the Dissolution of the Monasteries?

- Think of how the Dissolution of the Monasteries ended the support for the poor and sick that had been provided by religious houses. This led to increased hardship, poverty and vagrancy.
- Think of how the land and wealth of the monasteries was taken over by the King, who became much richer and spent some of the money on defence against invasion. Much land was also sold on to nobles and gentry, who became wealthier and more powerful as a result.
- Remember you need to go beyond the stimulus material provided by the two bullet points in the question. Were there other consequences of the dissolution of the monasteries and were these more important than the Pilgrimage of Grace?

Step 2: Identify

The 16-mark question requires you to reach a judgement on a statement. In order to do this effectively you need to identify **clear criteria** for reaching that judgement. Just like you need to cover a range of factors in 'explain' questions, you need to **cover a range of criteria** in 'judgement' questions.

Possible criteria for reaching a judgement:

- You could evaluate how wide-ranging the consequences were. Did the event have mainly financial/economic consequences or were there important political consequences as well?
- You could also analyse how many people were affected by the event. Did the disruption of economic life associated with the monasteries apply mainly to the north of England or did it affect the whole country?

Step 3: Organise

The simplest way to plan for judgement-style questions is to think in terms of 'for' and 'against' paragraphs:

- Paragraph 1 – Evidence to **support** the statement. For example, show how anger over the Dissolution of the Monasteries motivated people in the north of England to take up arms and defy the crown. This gave many an opportunity to voice their disquiet over other aspects of Henry's religious policies.
- Paragraph 2 – Evidence to **counter** the statement. Show how the the Pilgrimage of Grace was only a short-term consequence of the Dissolution. Other consequences were long term and had a permanent effect – for example, the monastic land sold by the crown gave the gentry more wealth and influence, and the destruction of buildings and art could never be reversed.
- Paragraph 3 – Your final conclusion. Weigh the evidence – how far do you agree with the statement?

Step 4: Prove

Remember to tie what you know to the question. Do not include information and think that it will speak for itself. Some students think that simply dropping examples in to the right paragraphs is enough. The following statement from a student could be further developed and gain more marks.

> *Another important consequence of the Dissolution of the Monasteries was that there was more poverty.*

This does not **prove** that increased poverty was a consequence of the Dissolution. The student needs to go on to explain **how** the Dissolution led to more poverty by explaining that many people lost their jobs in religious houses as cleaners or cooks, for example, or working on monastery farmland and that there were no longer monks and nuns providing food and money for those in need of help.

Step 5: Conclude

Your conclusion is a crucial part of your answer. You have been asked to reach a judgement on a statement. You need to state clearly how far you agree with it and your reason why. It would be easy to sit on the fence and avoid reaching a final conclusion. But sitting on the fence is a dangerous position. Your answer collapses and you lose marks.

Instead of sitting on the fence, you need to be confident and reach an overall judgement. Imagine that you have placed the evidence on a set of scales. How far do they tip in favour of the statement or against it?

You can then move on in your conclusion to explain your judgement. Do not repeat everything you have already written. Think of the scales – what are the heaviest pieces of evidence on each side? Build these into your conclusion in the following way:

Advice	Model
JUDGEMENT – Start with your judgement – try to incorporate words from the question into this sentence.	To a large extent, I agree that the Pilgrimage of Grace was a dangerous challenge to Henry VIII's power and authority. It was the most serious rebellion of his reign.
COUNTER – Show that you are aware that there is some evidence to counter this and give the best example.	Serious as it was, the Pilgrimage of Grace ultimately failed to change Henry's polices. The Dissolution of the Monasteries continued. Other consequences may not have been as dramatic, but they were more long lasting.
SUPPORT – Explain why, overall, you have reached the judgement you have. Give your key reason or reasons why.	The most important consequence of the Dissolution of the Monasteries was probably the way it transferred power and wealth from the Church into the hands of lords and gentlemen. This meant that the new owners of the lands and wealth of the Church were much less likely to oppose Henry VIII's religious changes. In the long run this was more significant than the fact that there was a rebellion which failed in 1536.

Practice questions

You can find further 'judgement' practice questions on pages 30, 43, 59, 74, 91 and 100

REMEMBER

Two important warnings.

Firstly, leave enough time to **check your answer** carefully for spelling, punctuation and grammar.

- Is your spelling and punctuation accurate?
- Does your work make sense? Are your arguments clear?
- Have you used a wide range of historical terms?

Secondly, **beware of iceberg questions**!

(c)(ii) 'His arrangement of Henry's marriage to Anne of Cleves was the main reason for the downfall of Thomas Cromwell in 1540.' How far do you agree? Explain your answer.

(16 marks)

Spot the part of the question that lurks beneath the water. Remember what we said about de-coding judgement questions like the one above (see page 74). You need to weigh the importance of the cause in the question against the importance of other causes (such as accusations of heresy against Cromwell, opposition from nobles at Court like the Duke of Norfolk, and Henry's character).

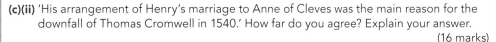

What are the key ingredients of effective writing in GCSE History?

The language you use to express your ideas is very important. One of the ways to get better at History is to be more precise with your use of language. For example, rather than simply saying that you **agree** or **disagree** with a statement you can use language that shows whether you agree to **a large extent** or only **to some extent**. Look at the different shades of argument below and experiment with using some of the phrases. Use them when you are debating or discussing in class.

Thinking carefully about the language you use

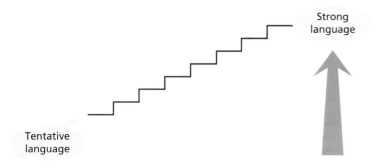

Varying your language to show how far you agree with a statement:	Varying your language to show how important a factor/cause is:
I totally/entirely/completely/absolutely agree with…	…was by far the most important reason why…
I substantially/fundamentally/strongly agree with…	The key/crucial/essential factor was…
I agree to a large extent with…	…was the main cause of…
I mainly/mostly agree with…	The most influential cause was…
I agree to some extent with…	…played a significant/important/major role in…
I partially/partly agree with…	…was of some importance in…
I only agree with … to a limited/slight extent.	
Varying your language to show the significance or importance of an individual, discovery, event or development:	**Varying your language to show the extent of change:**
…made the most important/significant contribution to…	…was revolutionised in…
…had a crucial/major/highly significant impact on…	…totally changed during…
…had an important/influential impact on…	…was transformed during…
…was of some importance/significance to…	…there was fundamental change in…
…only made a limited/partial/slight/minimal contribution to…	The period saw significant/important progress in…
	…saw some changes in…
	…saw some progress in…
	…saw limited/slight/minimal progress in…

Helpful phrases and sentence starters		
When you want to explore the other side of an argument:	**When you want to highlight similarities:**	**When you want to make an additional point to support an argument:**
On the other hand…	In the same way…	Also… Additionally… In addition…
However…	Similarly… This is similar to the way that…	Moreover…
Alternatively, it could be argued that…	Likewise…	Furthermore…
When you want to link points or show that one thing led to another:	**When you want to give examples to support a point:**	**When you want to show that an individual, event or discovery was important:**
Therefore…	For example… For instance…	…was a crucial turning point in…
Due to…	This can be seen when…	…acted as an important catalyst for…
Consequently…	This is clearly shown by…	Without this event/development/ discovery … would not have happened.
One consequence of this was…	This is supported by…	This had an immediate impact on…
This caused…	This is proven by…	In the short term this transformed/ revolutionised…
This led to…		In the long term this had a lasting impact on…
This resulted in…		
This meant that…		

You can use the **progression grid** below to get an idea of what getting better at history looks like. This is designed to give you a general idea of what you need to do to produce good answers in the exam. It focuses on the four key things in the coloured squares on the bingo card on page 122.

		Question focus	Organisation	Line of argument	Supporting information
High level		The answer is consistently focused on the question.	The answer is structured very carefully and explanations are coherent throughout.	The line of argument is very clear and convincing. It flows throughout the answer.	Supporting information has been precisely selected and shows wide-ranging knowledge and understanding.
		The answer is mainly focused on the question.	The answer is well organised but some parts lack coherence.	The line of argument is clear, convincing and generally maintained through the answer.	Supporting information is accurate and relevant and shows good knowledge and understanding.
		The answer has weak or limited links to the question.	Some statements are developed and there is some attempt to organise the material.	The line of argument is partly convincing but not maintained through the answer.	Supporting information is mainly accurate and relevant and shows some knowledge and understanding.
		The answer has no real links to the question.	The answer lacks organisation.	The line of argument is unclear or missing.	Supporting information is limited or not relevant.

Self-assessing and peer assessing your work

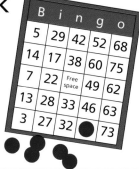

It is important that you check your own work before you hand it to your teacher to be marked. Sometimes you may be asked to assess the work of someone else in your class. In both cases you need to know what you are looking for. What are the key ingredients of great writing in History?

You can use the **bingo card** below as a checklist – get competitive and try to show that you have covered all the squares and got a full house of ingredients!

The answer starts with a **clear focus on the question** (there is no long introduction). Key words from the question are used during the answer. For longer answers, each paragraph is linked to the question.	Statements and arguments are fully developed and explained – showing good knowledge and understanding. Arguments are **well supported** by accurate, relevant and well-selected evidence.	**Connectives** are used to help prove arguments and show significance/impact. Look for phrases like: *this led to…* *this resulted in…* *this meant that…*
There is a **clear line of argument** at the start of each paragraph – think of it as a signpost for what follows. The rest of the paragraph supports this argument. The line of argument flows throughout the answer, building up to a clear conclusion.	Paragraphs have been used to provide a **clear structure**. Each paragraph starts with a different cause/factor (12-mark 'explain' questions) or a different theme/criteria (16-mark 'judgement' questions).	The answer shows **wide-ranging** knowledge and understanding. It considers a range of factors/causes ('explain' questions) or explores the evidence for **and** against a statement ('judgement' questions).
The language used helps to construct very precise arguments – showing how important the writer thinks a cause/factor, event or individual is. A good range of specialist **historical vocabulary** has been used.	There is a **clear conclusion**. For 'explain' questions factors/causes are prioritised or linked. For 'judgement' questions there is a focus on 'how far' the writer agrees with the statement.	The answer has been **carefully checked** for spelling, punctuation and grammar. The meaning is always clear throughout the answer.

Glossary

Abbot   The monk in charge of a monastery.

Accession   The act of becoming king.

Almoners   Monks who distributed charity to the poor.

Altar   The table at the centre of religious services, used for consecrating the bread and wine during holy communion.

Ambassador   A person sent to discuss important matters with the ruler of another country.

Annulment   Declaring that a marriage was not legal.

Apostles' Creed   A statement of what Christians believe.

Battle of Agincourt   The English victory over the French in 1415.

Benedictine   A member of the order of Benedictine monks.

Chancellor/Lord Chancellor   The king's chief secretary.

Chaplain   A priest who holds services for a king or nobleman and his family.

Chastity   Abstaining from marriage or sexual relations.

Chief Minister   The king's right-hand man, who supervised most of the government's work.

Cloisters   An enclosed area within a monastery consisting of a covered passageway surrounding an open space.

Court of Star Chamber   A special law court where the king could take cases from the common law courts and have them heard in secret.

Diplomacy   Relations between countries, usually conducted by ambassadors.

Diplomatic marriage   A marriage arranged to make an alliance between two different countries.

Dissolution of the Monasteries   The closure of the monasteries between 1536 and 1539, through which Henry VIII took their wealth.

Enclosures   Areas of farmland that were being fenced off for private use, often taken from common land.

Eucharist   The Christian ceremonial act of communion with God, in which bread and wine are taken to commemorate the Last Supper of Christ.

Forced Loan   Money which wealthy landowners and merchants were forced to lend to the government. They rarely got any of it back.

Heresy   Religious beliefs which go against the teachings of the Church.

Holy relics   Part of the body of a saint or other holy person, or an object belonging to a saint.

Holy Roman Empire   The German empire, governed by the Emperor.

Jousting tournaments   Competitions in which knights rode at each other with lances.

Knight of the Garter   A member of the Order of the Garter, a privileged group dedicated to chivalry.

Lord Protector   An emergency title given to a powerful figure when the king is a child or incapacitated.

Lord Treasurer   Member of the Royal Council in charge of the country's finances.

Lord's Prayer   'Our Father, who art in Heaven...' The prayer taught to the twelve Apostles by Jesus.

Magistrate   A person who takes part in local government.

Maid of honour   A woman who attends the queen.

Mass   The name given to the Communion Service by Catholics, where the priest spoke in Latin and communicants believed the bread and wine were transformed into the body and blood of Jesus.

Mercenary soldier   A soldier who fought for wages, sometimes in the army of a foreign country.

Merchants   People who were involved in trade – for example, exporting English wool to the continent.

Monastic schools   Schools within monasteries.

Monastic vows   The promises made by men and women on becoming monks and nuns, especially the promises to give up wealth (poverty), to live without sexual relations (chastity), and to obey the Church (obedience).

Monasticism   Having to do with monasteries, monks or nuns.

Papacy   The Pope and his territories – the Vatican in Rome and the Papal States in central Italy.

Patronage   The power to make appointments to government jobs.

Praemunire   The offence of asserting the power of a foreign prince in England.

Priory   A type of monastery.

Privy Council   The king's inner circle of advisers.

Purgatory   According to Catholic belief, the place where the souls of the dead await judgement before going to heaven or hell.

Reformation of the Church in England   The English Reformation: the period during which the English Church became Protestant.

Religious houses   Monasteries, priories, convents, abbeys.

Royal Council   Any council called to advise the king.

Saint   A person whom the Church has said lived a life of great holiness.

Salvation   Going to heaven.

Sanctuary   A place where the king's law-enforcement officers could not arrest you.

Solicitor-General   The king's chief law-enforcement officer.

Sovereignty   Independence; supreme power.

Succession   The order in which one person follows another to the throne.

Temporal prince   A secular ruler, rather than a religious one.

Ten Commandments   The ten fundamental religious laws brought down from Mount Sinai by Moses and given to the Israelites by God.

Treason   An attempt to overthrow the government of the state in which the offender owes allegiance.

Treason laws   Laws to punish treason.

Vice-Gerent in Spirituals   The title given to Thomas Cromwell by Henry VIII that gave him authority to supervise religious life in England.

Photo credits

The Publishers would like to thank the following for permission to reproduce copyright material.

p.3 © Topham Picturepoint/TopFoto; **p.8** © Keith Heron/Alamy Stock Photo; **p.11** © Hulton Archive/Getty Images; **p.13** © Print Collector/Hulton Fine Art Collection/ Getty Images; **p.18** © Granger, NYC./Alamy Stock Photo; **p.19** © Travel21 Impact/ Heritage Images/TopFoto; **pp.22–23** © Niday Picture Library/Alamy Stock Photo; **p.27** *l* © Portrait of Emperor Karl V, c.1540-45 (oil on panel), German School, (16th century)/ Germanisches Nationalmuseum, Nuremberg, Germany/Bridgeman Images; *m* © The Print Collector/HIP/TopFoto; *r* © Print Collector/Hulton Fine Art Collection/Getty Images; **p.33** © The Bodleian Library, University of Oxford, MS. Douce 363, fol. 091r; **p.34** © DEA/G. NIMATALLAH/De Agostini Picture Library/Getty Images; **p.35** © Fine Art Images/Heritage Images/TopFoto; **p.39** *l* © Heritage Image Partnership Ltd/Alamy Stock Photo; *r* ©The Granger Collection/TopFoto; **p.41** © Henry VIII (1491–1547), Cleve, Joos van (c.1485–1541)/Burghley House Collection, Lincolnshire, UK/Bridgeman Images; **p.46** © PAINTING/Alamy Stock Photo; **p.47** © IanDagnall Computing/Alamy Stock Photo; **p.56** © Ann Ronan Picture Library/Heritage Images/TopFoto; **p.60** © Roger-Viollet/ TopFoto; **p.61** *t* © World History Archive/TopFoto; *b* © English School/Getty Images; **p.64** © Julian Eales/Alamy Stock Photo; **p.68** © IanDagnall Computing/Alamy Stock Photo; **p.72** © Ivy Close Images/Alamy Stock Photo; **p.77** © Everett Collection Historical/ Alamy Stock Photo; **p.82** © Holbein the Younger, Hans (1497/8-1543) (after)/Private Collection/The Stapleton Collection/Bridgeman Images; **p.83** © World History Archive/ TopFoto; **p.85** © Lebrecht Music and Arts Photo Library/Alamy Stock Photo; **p.90** © World History Archive/TopFoto; **p.92** © Anna Stowe/Alamy Stock Photo; **pp.94–95** © York Museums Trust; **p.98** © Ian Dagnall/Alamy Stock Photo; **p.101** © Badge of the Five Wounds of Christ (embroidered textile), English School, (16th century)/His Grace The Duke of Norfolk, Arundel Castle/Bridgeman Images; **p.104** © Pontefract Castle, c.1620-40, Keirincx, Alexander (1600-c.1652)/Wakefield Museums and Galleries, West Yorkshire, UK/ Bridgeman Images; **p.108** © Massys, Cornelis (1508-80)/National Portrait Gallery, London, UK/Bridgeman Images; **p.110** © Topham Picturepoint/TopFoto.

Index